T0269908

PRAISE FOR
NIGHTLIFE LESSONS

"I've been working in venture and technology for a long time. What Shane and his team were able to do, in terms of re-inventing the business of nightlife, is a fantastic example for entrepreneurs and investors at all levels. Each 'nightlife lesson' is a gem."

HOWARD MORGAN
founder of First Round Capital and Chairman of B Capital

"The essence of nightlife is pushing boundaries while having a great time, and Shane Neman lived that out in one of the industry's most interesting periods: the late '90s and early '00s. His book is a real insider's take on those years, which makes it a fun read—but it's also a revelation, the story of how the mechanics of nightlife completely transformed, largely because of Shane and his team. For anyone who wants to know more about business, technology, and the nightlife biz itself, this book delivers."

STEVE LEWIS
"Godfather of NYC Nightlife"

"I've been a technology business investor for many decades and Shane has truly captured the essence of entrepreneurship in *Nightlife Lessons* in a way no other book has. If you want to learn about grit, hard work, and innovation, then this book succeeds, with a generous dose of humor and entertainment that won't put you to sleep like most other cliché business books."

HENRY KRESSEL
engineer of the first fiber optic laser and partner at Warburg Pincus

"Like a delirious night of clubbing, *Nightlife Lessons* gives you the ups and downs of the entrepreneurial life from someone who has lived it up close and shaped its evolution for more than two decades. Shane Neman uses his past leveraging of technology to help you understand the industry as well as the continuing value and tech revolution coming in the future."

JEFF GROSS
professional poker player

"*Nightlife Lessons* is an engaging walk down the best of memory lane, but more importantly, it's a story that exemplifies positive disruption and the redefining of an industry. As a seasoned hospitality investor, I highly recommend it!"

MARC BELL
financier and entrepreneur; CEO and founder, Terran Orbital

"Shane is one of the best storytellers I know. I can listen to (or read) him endlessly. *Nightlife Lessons* is packed with creative and helpful advice from the perspective of a tech-nerd-turned-entrepreneur in a dynamic industry. This book reads so smoothly you'll wish the night went on longer when you reach the end."

DARIUS FOROUX
author of *Think Straight* and *Do It Today*

"*Nightlife Lessons* is a highly readable return to New York City in the 1990s, through the lens of the city's legendary club scene. My friend of many years, Shane Neman, explains how he built not just a business but a tech enterprise during those years. An insightful book with lessons for entrepreneurs, investors, and nightlife aficionados alike."

RONN TOROSSIAN
founder and CEO of 5WPR

NIGHTLIFE LESSONS

www.amplifypublishinggroup.com

Nightlife Lessons: How I Conquered the Business of Partying with Tech and a Glimpse into Its Future

For more information, please contact:
Amplify Publishing, an imprint of Amplify Publishing Group
620 Herndon Parkway, Suite 320
Herndon, VA 20170
info@amplifypublishing.com

Library of Congress Control Number: 2023901529

CPSIA Code: PRV0323A

ISBN-13: 978-1-63755-681-8

Printed in the United States

To my mom, Guita Neman, who through her own grit, hard work, and perseverance convinced me throughout my life that I can accomplish anything.

NIGHT
LIFE
LESSONS

How I Conquered the Business of Partying with Tech and a Glimpse into Its Future

SHANE NEMAN

an imprint of Amplify Publishing Group

CONTENTS

PREFACE

Getting In

ON NEW YEAR'S EVE, 1990, I got my first taste of a New York City nightclub. I was only in eighth grade then: a young Jewish kid, born in Brooklyn, and living in the Long Island suburbs. But that one foray into the world of nightlife was the turning point that put me on the path to success. In the unlikely ecosystem of NYC nightlife, I learned invaluable lessons that allowed me to build not one, but two incredibly successful startups from the ground up. Those experiences also have given me a unique perspective as a venture capitalist when I back fledgling companies and entrepreneurs. This book explains those lessons in detail. My hope is that it will help other entrepreneurs on the path to success, and that we'll have some fun along the way.

New York Legends

NYC nightlife in the nineties was legendary. Cutting-edge music pulsated through outrageously themed rooms in cavernous, multilevel mega-clubs such as Limelight, Palladium, and Club USA. Mobs of people lined up outside, eager to experience life outside normal, everyday boundaries.

The typical crowd at this kind of club was eclectic in the extreme, a brash mix of stereotypes—iconic, costumed Club Kids, drug-addled ravers, Eurotrash, drag queens, "bridge-and-tunnel" New Yorkers (non-Manhattanites who would come in from the outer boroughs), the gays and lesbians, downtown art hipsters, waiflike heroin-chic models, yuppies, preppies that went to the NYC "Ivy League" high schools like Dalton and Riverdale, Wall Street suits, and of course, celebrities.

It was unreal to walk into a club crowded with all these people, getting a chance to experience each other, learn from each other, and have fun with each other. There was nowhere else you could find this kind of diversity, chaos, and creativity. It was as though society itself had been amplified and turned in a kaleidoscope.

Old for My Age

Fourteen was young to go party at a club like that, but as far back as I can remember, most of my friends were older kids, usually by several years. Maybe it was because I was tall, or maybe I acted mature for my age. In any case, some of my older friends got their hands on VIP tickets for a club called Elements on New Year's Eve, 1990. They offered tickets to me and a couple of other kids my age in our friend group, and we took them up on it, hardly believing our good luck.

A few nights before the party, one of the guys drove to my house to drop off my ticket. I met Mayer outside and gave him seventy-five bucks for it, which was more than half my savings.

The ticket itself was thin white cardstock. "New Year's Eve 1990" and the Elements logo were stamped on it in glittery, old-style cursive. Underneath were the words "Admit One - VIP (21 and Over)." I couldn't take my eyes off it!

I asked my mom for permission to buy the ticket and go. Even though I was only in eighth grade, my mom didn't give me a hard time. She knew I was a responsible, preppy, and even geeky kid—not the type to look for trouble—and trusted me to be careful. I gave her the names and phone numbers of everyone I was going with, and she gave me a ride to the train station and a mini-lecture on safe sex and the dangers of drugs and alcohol.

My mom was always super open about things like that, which was something I really appreciated. But to be honest, I wasn't even close to experimenting with those things at that age. Even when I was in college and frequented clubs like SpyBar, Life, Au Bar, Cheetah, Veruka, and Suite 16, I never got into drug use or heavy drinking. Plus, as a teenager in middle and high school, just the cost of getting into clubs on a regular basis really added up. I didn't have the money to play around with those kinds of experiences! So, I went through the '90s' club scene without getting into the harder side of things, and in fact, was often oblivious to it.

As I handed over the seventy-five dollars, and received my ticket in return, I asked about a worry that had been nagging at me since I heard about the party. Would this even work? Would I actually be able to get *into* the club? Sure, I was old for my age, but still—I was only fourteen. Mayer brushed away my concerns.

"Don't worry, Shag," he said, grinning. ("Shag" had been my

nickname since elementary school, because of my shaggy haircut.) "Just say you're with Fred Asher's group. He's the one throwing the party. You're in good hands. You're gonna have the time of your life." He threw his car into gear and started driving away, tossing a final word of encouragement over his shoulder: "This is going to be the best party NYC has ever seen! Trust me!"

Getting In

I got to the station at about seven thirty that night. Figuring out what to wear had been a real problem; the only clothes I had for parties were a suit and tie that my mom had bought me to wear to friends' bar mitzvahs. In the end, I decided to go with as simple an outfit as possible: black jeans, a black Honest Belt with a silver buckle, and a black Hanes T-shirt with the sleeves rolled up precisely two folds. Black suede Dr. Martens and my Schott leather bomber jacket completed the look. It was as cool as I was going to get.

Cool was right. This was New York in December, and I was *freezing*.

But looking the part, or at least trying to, was way more important than being warm! I joined my friends, feeling super excited in spite of the cold, and we all huddled into a circle, trying to keep warm. Everyone was talking loudly and giving each other high fives. We were sure there was a great night in store for us, and the anticipation was exhilarating.

The excitement stayed with us through the entire forty-minute train ride to Manhattan. Some of the older guys had brought mixed drinks with them in water bottles and were already getting started on their night of hard partying. Others, like me, were just happy to be along for the ride—that was a big enough high for us!

Another freezing wait in the cold, a quick cab ride, and we were finally at the club. From the outside, Elements looked like nothing more than a big warehouse in a seedy part of town, slightly graffiti-ed and situated on a nondescript, even desolate street. And although the event was supposed to start in five minutes, there was nobody outside except us. Typical rookie mistake.

Awkwardly, we lined up alongside some velvet ropes leading to the open, pullback gate. After about ten frigid minutes, a tall, good-looking European man came out. This was the era of doormen: enigmatic, powerful, and often eccentric characters in the nightclub ecosystem. Some of them, like Kenny Kenny (a cross-dressing Irishman with an outrageous life-as-art wardrobe and an even wilder attitude) and Aphrodita (who really did look like a Greek goddess but was in fact a sixteen-year-old girl with a penchant for '70s fashion), became celebrities in their own right. They were literally the gatekeepers to that world!

"Can I help you?" the doorman asked.

In unison, we all produced our white tickets and started explaining that we were with Fred. For some reason, this caused him to roll his eyes and sigh. He glanced at our tickets, and then told us disdainfully that we were in the wrong line. "This is for the General," he said, indicating the line we were standing in, on the right side of the door. "You need to be in the VIP line." He gestured toward the line we were apparently supposed to be in.

We looked at each other. The "line" he was pointing toward consisted of another set of velvet ropes, on the opposite side of the same door, a few feet from where we were standing. Both lines led to exactly the same place.

Not knowing any better, we awkwardly filed out of the General Admission line and around to the VIP side, where we waited, shivering, for another fifteen minutes while he pretended to be busy and fussed with a clipboard. Finally, he took our tickets, grudgingly removed the ropes across the entrance, and let us inside.

It was a relief to be warm, and an even bigger relief to have gotten past the door! The first thing we did was troop to the coat-check area and hand our coats and jackets to the woman working there. She gave us each a red bracelet, explaining that they gave us access to the open bar and VIP areas. I was so excited that I gave her my jacket and then walked away to explore without waiting for my coat check ticket. She had to chase me down and give it to me!

For about an hour, my friends and I were the only people in the whole joint. It made things kind of strange, but the music, lights, and whole atmosphere were enough for us to be more than happy. For me especially, the experience of being in the city without my parents, in an amazing nightclub (where I was technically not even allowed to be), made me feel super cool and grown-up.

Eventually, people started showing up, and it seemed like every person who walked in was more gorgeous, stylish, and sophisticated than the one before. The men were all handsome, the women were all super-hot, and everyone was much older than we were—they were adults! All of them were wearing jaw-dropping evening wear, some of it ultra-formal and some of it outrageous and funky. These were clothes that were obviously haute couture, or else the latest thing by some up-and-coming designer no one had even heard about yet.

It was an eye-opening sight, and I realized that compared to these partygoers, my friends and I all looked like big *duds*. Oh well, I thought. At least I hadn't gone with the dorky bar mitzvah suit, as some of my friends unfortunately had. Either way, it wasn't going to faze me: I was determined to have an awesome night.

In the House

We decided to split up into two- and three-person groups to explore. My friend Miron and I teamed up, pushing our way through the growing crowd to get to—well, we didn't know where, exactly, but to get *somewhere*. We left the bar, with its chill electronic and pop music, and soon found ourselves in an all-black room with a seamy, grimy vibe and hip-hop music pounding through the sound system.

That room was fun, and we hung around for a little while, dancing a bit to some of the songs we liked. When we started to get bored, we headed downstairs, where we found a much smaller area with just a dance floor. The DJ was blasting house music, and the strobe lights flashed to the beat.

Until then, I had been veering between extremes of feeling incredibly excited to be somewhere so out of my league, and feeling incredibly out of place, sipping at a Sprite and pretending it was a vodka soda. Basically, I had no idea what I was doing. Miron, on the other hand, was downing beers with a certain amount of expertise; even though we were the same age, he was fairly experienced at getting drunk and was already on his fifth beer or so.

But when we got to that room, all my concerns about fitting in melted away as I listened to the music. At that time (and sometimes even now), my favorite music was deep vocal house, and the songs the DJ played were like nothing I had ever heard. I made a mental note to ask him where I could buy songs like that, because they definitely weren't available at the Tower Records I went to.

At that precise moment, through the darkness, strobe lights, and music, someone grabbed me by the front of my shirt and pulled me forward. Suddenly I found myself dancing, *very* closely, with a tall, beautiful blonde. Like me, she was dressed all in black: a silk top, leather pants, and a bomber jacket much like the one I had checked at the entrance. She was alluring, sophisticated, and seemed a lot more mature than I was. Looking back, I guess she was probably only a girl in her early twenties, but to me at that time, she was a woman!

It took me a moment to take stock of the situation and calm my nerves. I played it cool and concentrated on dancing with her. After a minute, I tried to say something—but I could hardly hear myself over the music, let alone what she said in reply. I just kept nodding my head, trying to keep things flowing. The most important thing was for this experience not to end.

Looking around for Miron, I saw that he was in the same position as I was, dancing with another girl who seemed to be friends with the one I was dancing with. I chuckled inside, feeling happy for him.

To my complete shock, as I turned back to my dance partner, she pulled my shirt again, and this time she was coming in close for a kiss. I couldn't believe what was happening. But I went with it, and our passionate kiss lasted what felt like fifteen minutes.

I was on a major endorphin high when the kiss ended, but another curve ball was coming. Her friend suddenly left Miron and stalked over to us, grabbed my dance partner by the hand and dragged her away. They left abruptly, with no time for goodbyes or even exchanging names. I was in shock all over again, crashing from elation to utter disappointment.

But nothing could bother me for long. Miron and I looked at each other, knowing that what had just happened was many teenage boys' dream come true. We gave each other a big hug and high-five. Then, grinning ear to ear, I went to the DJ booth, my adrenaline still pumping, and asked the DJ about the last few songs. Carelessly, he flipped me a cassette tape of his most recent mix, saying that all the songs I had just heard were on it. It was the ultimate cherry on top.

A Substance-Free Bender

At about five in the morning, we all finally found each other in the rapidly emptying club and made our way outside into the frigid gusts of winter. Feverishly talking over each other the entire time, we waited for cabs and went back to Penn Station, where we boarded the train and headed home. That train ride was one long competition. Everyone wanted to be the first to get their story out, and each person had had something funny or crazy to tell, from hooking up with a girl like Miron and I had, to meeting a celebrity, or passing out drunk for half the night, only to wake up in the bathroom.

From the raucous reactions of our group, it was clear that Miron and I had the greatest tale to tell—everyone was enthralled with our story! They were all asking me to make copies of the tape the DJ had given me, and I could hardly wait to go home and play it on my stereo. (I didn't have a TV in my room at that time, but I did have my own boombox stereo!)

We were amped up all the way back to Long Island, and some of us were crashing at our friend Ramie's apartment. The apartment belonged to his parents who had been doing some construction there, and almost all the furniture was gone. But we didn't care. We rolled up our jackets for pillows and lay on the floor, still too exhilarated to sleep.

It was about noon when my mom came to pick me up. She was full of questions. How did I feel? How was the party? Had it been fun? But by then, exhaustion was setting in, and all I could manage were terse, one-word answers: fine, good, yes, no, OK.

As always, my mom was very understanding, and let me be. I was thankful to her for that because it was starting to feel like my brain might melt. Once we got home, I ate a big bowl of spaghetti with homemade Bolognese sauce and headed to my room. I fell asleep walking up the stairs.

The clock said seven when I finally woke up. It was dark outside, obviously evening; I made my way downstairs, where my mom asked again how I was feeling and how the party had gone. This time, I was wide awake, and told her all about it—how much fun everyone had, how great the music was, how cool the club was, how the doorman treated us, how we were so noisy and laughed so much on the train ride home, and how there was no furniture at Ramie's house. The only thing I left out was the part about making out with the hot blonde ten years older than I was. That seemed like a detail best kept private.

It felt great to relive my adventure, and when I was done, there was a contented silence. Then my mom asked me when I was going to get my homework done. I looked at her strangely. "Why would I be doing homework on Saturday night?" I asked.

Now it was her turn to look at me strangely.

"My love ..." she said, "It's *Sunday* night. You've been asleep since we got home yesterday. I checked on you a few times, but you were sleeping so soundly, I just let you be."

I went from feeling happy to shocked and then super-bummed. What a moment to have to sit down and get started on homework! I'd had my first bender at the age of fourteen, without getting drunk, or high, or even knowing what the word "bender" meant. And I lost a whole day of my life sleeping it off.

But it was a night I would never forget. New Year's Eve of 1990 sparked in me an insatiable taste for the gritty, chaotic whirl of NYC nightlife, which would last through high school, college, and beyond. Even after graduation, I was a regular at Pangaea, Rehab, Marquee, Cain, and other hotspots.

Nightlife, in turn, would provide a springboard for big lessons in my professional life, which made it possible for me to succeed beyond all my expectations—first with JoonBug, a company that created a suite of software solutions that brought event marketing and promotions into the digital age. JoonBug was the first to build a technology stack that included digital photo purchasing and social sharing, e-ticketing systems, and targeted email newsletters. In a period of eight years, I built JoonBug to over $25 million in annual revenues.

Afterward, I put those same lessons to work at EZ Texting, an online SMS messaging platform for businesses. EZ Texting rapidly grew to annual revenues in the high seven figures before its acquisition by CallFire in 2013.

Now, I'm a prolific venture capitalist, backing a diverse set of startups, as well as a real estate investor managing a portfolio of more than twenty properties in major metropolitan areas across the U.S. And yes, I am still indebted to, and reaping the benefits from, those first invaluable nightlife lessons.

INTRODUCTION

You've Been Bitten by the JoonBug

THE WORLD OF NIGHTLIFE IS a world of mystery, chaos, and potential. The people and the experiences associated with that two-in-the-morning existence just seem to produce electric, out-of-the-box ideas.

I have seen the nightlife industry propel some of the more interesting characters in entrepreneurship not only to stardom but to great wealth. For me personally, the nightclub and events scene in New York City proved to be a steppingstone to success in my career, as well as in my personal life.

The Lowest Point

It was late 2001, just after 9/11. Americans, especially New Yorkers, were reeling from that shocking national tragedy; no one really knew how to process the horrible events that had just taken place.

Depression and confusion were almost tangible, like a dismal fog everywhere you went.

It was also around this time that the tech bubble burst, and like many other entrepreneurs in the tech industry, I found myself out of a job. Despite having a viable and innovative product, enthusiastic investors, and an engaged customer base, the tech startup Offyx I had founded with my friend Jon went bust during the dot-com crash.

All of this came on the heels of a long, draining period in my life. I had worked obsessively to get into medical school, only to realize that, as much as becoming a doctor had been my dream, it was a career that made me miserable. The decision to drop out had been agonizing.

That was also the same period in which my mom had suffered a debilitating stroke. Thankfully, she partially recovered, becoming self-sufficient once more, but it was a very hard time not only for her, but for me as I cared for her in the years of recovery.

Lightbulb Moment

I had no particular place to go. Nothing to do. It was my lowest point, and in the vacuum, late nights became commonplace. I found myself sitting in club after club, night after night, thinking things over. And during that time, I noticed something.

Club owners and promoters were busy doing whatever they could to attract crowds and sell tickets. But as I sat watching them, I began to notice that most of their efforts seemed ineffective, even backward. They were printing flyers and mailing them, or, worse, handing them out—to distracted, tired, or just plain drunk patrons leaving the club! One guess as to where those flyers went: right into the gutter, or the trash if they were lucky.

Club owners and promoters also employed "list-girls." These girls were tasked with carrying clipboards around the club each evening, asking patrons for their phone numbers, and writing them down by hand. The following day, cold-callers would call those numbers and invite the people on the other line to more events. It all seemed very outdated and unevolved; I couldn't imagine the system was cost-effective, or the success rate very good.

I also discovered that there was not a single website online where you could do a quick, basic search of what was happening on a given night in New York City. With that realization, all the pieces fell into place. I decided that bringing club promotions into the modern, digital world would be my next business.

Nobody Knows Like Guastavino's

At that time, I was dating a girl named Ariana Gordon (now Ariana Stecker). She and I were both from Great Neck and had a ton of friends in common, but she had gone to North High while I went to South High, and somehow, we'd never met until we were in our twenties. Appropriately enough, we first met at a club.

My friend Craig Koenig was head promoter of a club called Opera in West Chelsea, and Ariana regularly worked the door there while attending the Fashion Institute of Technology. I started going to Opera every Saturday night, and more often than not ended up hanging out with Ariana outside of the club in the early morning hours, when everyone had left.

Before long, we were seriously dating. A short time later, my friend Jon and I launched our tech startup, Offyx, while Ariana graduated and went to work for The Miami Project for Curing Paralysis, organizing big fundraisers like celebrity events and auctions.

When Offyx went bust, I went broke, and Ariana and I moved in together. We rented a small studio apartment on 58th Street, between First and Second Avenue, sharing the rent to make things easier on both of us.

The first night of living in our new place, we took a walk around the neighborhood. Our walk led us underneath the 59th Street Bridge, where we were amazed to find something neither of us expected: a gigantic, gorgeous restaurant, built right into the arches of the bridge. It was called Guastavino's, and it is still up and running as a luxury event space in NYC.

It was brand new, with a sleekness of design that rivaled the best venues either of us had ever seen. Obviously, it had cost millions to build out, but bizarrely, neither Ariana nor I, with our years of experience and extensive contacts in NYC nightlife, had any idea that it existed.

I looked at Ariana. "We should do a party over here!" I said. "I can't believe nobody knows about this place—it's probably the sickest venue in all of NYC right now!"

For a week, we walked past Guastavino's every night. And each time we passed by, it was basically empty, even on the weekend. Granted, it would have been hard to fill it up; even with 1,500 people inside, the place was just so big that it would still look empty.

As we staked it out, the vision became clearer and clearer. Ariana and I would throw a Halloween party there, which would fit the look of the place very well. And we would be able to pack it, because absolutely everyone went out on Halloween. The only question was, "How?"

JoonBug Is Born

Together, Ariana and I worked and planned and held our first event at Guastavino's. Innovating and evolving club promotions was going to be my new business, and this was my first shot at it. My idea was to create a website to promote the party, and to hand out special invitations that would direct users to our website.

To register the site, I needed to think of a name. In the 1990s and early 2000s, as new tech companies popped up everywhere, rocketed to fame, fizzled out, and generally became a whole new industry, naming startups was less of an art than a guessing game. Many of the most successful ones had odd (but catchy) names that really had nothing to do with the businesses themselves: think Yahoo, Google, Amazon, and many more.

I came up with "JoonBug" while on a phone call with my uncle Payam. As he and I chatted about this and that, I overheard his wife, Meredith, ask him something. As always, she called him "joonbug."

It was a special nickname she'd made up. In Farsi, "joon" is a common endearment meaning "my life" or "my soul." Meredith didn't speak Farsi, but she'd picked up the term and made it her own, combining it with "June bug." It was cute, catchy, and unusual. I instantly thought, "That's it!"

A few clicks later and I had joonbug.com registered with Network Solutions, the only domain registrar around at the time. I tried to buy junebug.com as well, in case of misspellings, but it was already taken. Still, having one of the two domain names was good enough.

Then I had to build the website and design a logo. Building the website I could do, for sure, but the logo was a lot trickier. In spite of all the programming I could churn out and the sophisticated code I could write, I was a complete dope when it came to graphic design. However, with a budget of zero dollars, I had to go with whatever I could manage to make on my own. No hiring, no purchasing, and unfortunately, no surplus of YouTube tutorials like there are today!

With "JoonBug" in mind, I envisioned a ladybug, and drew a circle using the circle tool. Then I drew a straight black line across the circle near the top, for the ladybug's head. Another straight line down the middle separated the wings. I added small circles here and there, filled with black, for the ladybug spots. Finally, I filled the rest in with red. Voilà! A logo that was simple, workable, and best of all: free!

Now I could get into the nitty gritty of the actual website. In its early stages, joonbug.com had only two sections, one for photos and one for events. In time, as JoonBug grew from a simple website to an events powerhouse, we would add sections for digital ticket sales (long before Eventbrite), photo sales, ads, and even a dating app! But the real lifeblood of JoonBug was on the backend of the website: our database of subscribers. The Guastavino's party alone earned us tens of thousands of subscribers. From there, the number only grew!

Why Own the Club When You Can Own the Tech?

The heart of JoonBug's success was simple: while the rest of the nightlife world was focused on bottles and models, we were focused on data and tech. When I walked into a party, I didn't see a thousand people in a club. Instead, I saw a market segment, part of a much larger network of millions, that could be monetized digitally.

For us, it didn't matter how much you were spending on Grey Goose, it mattered that you connected with us so that we could keep you in the loop. If you were invited to Butter on a Monday night by a promoter, you were only helping the owners of Butter make a profit. But if you were part of the JoonBug database, we could invite you to the hottest events at Butter, Marquee, TenJune, Pacha, and everywhere else.

To build JoonBug, I wasn't sitting in the back of a club, surrounded by models drinking vodka and Red Bull. I was hustling around from club to club until four in the morning, and then getting to the office by nine to make sure that my employees were at work and the previous night's photos were uploaded on time. The club owners may have had the monopoly on celebrities, high rollers, athletes, media, and VIPs, but we controlled the masses—and that's where the money came from.

Our Guastavino's Halloween party amassed a database of over 25,000 young, urban professionals. Over the next five years, Joon-Bug's database grew to over a million subscribers, all people with a ton of disposable income who went out regularly in NYC. That was, and is, a very important demographic for a lot of companies, so you can imagine how major brands like Johnnie Walker and Mercedes loved us! We had the attention of one of their most elusive audiences, and that audience was literally opting in to hear what JoonBug had to say.

With our database and stratification techniques, we could fill places as small as fifty guests, all the way to tens of thousands. We could segment our information based on demographic data like age, sex, musical taste, disposable income, and favorite places to go out, chopping up the data to target the exact audience the event was trying to reach.

For example, we worked with Johnnie Walker to target men between the ages of 25 and 35 who made over a $100,000 annual salary and lived in NYC. Those guys in our database would be sectioned out for special invites to Johnnie Walker tasting events. Or when designers had sample sales in NYC, we would target the women they wanted to reach. And by emailing the people in our database who liked a certain type of music, we could sell out huge raves.

As our website traffic exploded, we were able to employ over a hundred photographers around the city, selling digital and print copies of their work, and all of this was way before Snapfish or camera phones were a thing. At that time, decent digital cameras cost thousands of dollars!

We expanded into new markets as well, covering events in other major cities, and marketed an email newsletter that gave our subscribers the latest info on nightlife possibilities. Club owners and promoters paid to be included in our newsletter, and corporate sponsors from Mercedes to American Express lined up to put ads on our website.

Our digital ticketing system allowed us to sell tens of millions of dollars in high-priced tickets in the cities we covered. By the time I sold the company, we were doing hundreds of events in New York City alone, from clubs such as Capitale, Marquee, and Cain to family venues such as Dave & Buster's in Times Square.

Everyone else? Still writing down names and numbers on sheets of paper.

HOW TO BE FAKE

WHEN IT COMES TO NIGHTLIFE, you're only as good as your last party. But when you're just starting out, you don't have a "last party" to point back to. Where does that leave you?

Answer: Calling, emailing, texting, and spending every bit of energy you have on promoting an event that may end up a catastrophe. It's hard not to be overwhelmed during the crucial startup phase.

Persistence Beats Resistance

At least, that was how it was for me during the months leading up to our first big party on Halloween at Guastavino's. Ariana and I had scoped the place out carefully, talked it over, and finally committed to the idea. I designed the JoonBug website and logo. Now it was time to put our plan into action, beginning with the most intimidating part: approaching Guastavino's.

It was going to be challenging no matter how we sliced it. One reason, of course, was that we were total unknowns. It was true that Ariana was a professional events coordinator for a big non-profit—The Miami Project to Cure Paralysis—and both of us had lived and breathed nightlife for years. We were friends with DJs, promoters, and doormen across the city. And Ariana had worked the door at some of the hottest clubs in Manhattan. Still, when it came to putting on our *own* events, we were nobodies.

On top of that, we were broke. Nonprofits don't typically pay a whole lot to freshly minted college grads like Ariana, and I had been out of work since Offyx had gone under. We were renting an apartment together and getting by, but that was all. We couldn't go dumping upfront money into an expensive event like the one we had in mind. It just wasn't going to happen. We would have to fake it until we could (hopefully) make it.

Puttin' On the Ritz

All the details of a big event are important, but none as important as the venue. If you don't have a venue, you don't have an event. So how was I supposed to book Guastavino's, a multimillion-dollar restaurant that had obviously been built with New York's biggest spenders in mind?

Well, it wouldn't happen at all without a phone call and a proposal. The first step, as far as I could tell, was to create a knockout proposal that would look absolutely legit. To get an idea of what that should look like, I asked Ariana for copies of proposals that the Miami Project sent to venues they wanted to book. These gave me a template for drafting my own.

I have to say that learning mundane things like how to use headers and footers in Word can really pay off sometimes. Positioning my newly created JoonBug logo in the header, I got to work making a professional letterhead for the proposal. In a risky move, I decided to add the prestigious 5th Avenue address of the office I had used in the Offyx days. I included the old Offyx fax number, too. It would be terrible if we got caught somehow, but I figured no one was going to be sending me things in the mail or by fax anytime soon. For JoonBug's main phone line, I used my own cell number.

Next, I wrote a little paragraph about JoonBug that was a complete and total fabrication: I claimed that we had been in business for over three years, and that we had put on events at places such as Au Bar, Suite 16, Cipriani, and a few other hotspots that I thought sounded impressive. The closest that was to the truth was that Ariana had worked the door at some of those places, and we had both gone to parties there over the years. Next, I added some information about Ariana's events background and my software background, and then got into the proposal itself.

I wrote that we were planning a 3,000-person Halloween party on October 31, 2001. That would be a Wednesday, which I hoped would make things easier. Wednesdays are usually slower nights for most restaurants and event spaces compared to the busier Thursday through Sunday nights.

I asked for a two-hour open bar, Halloween decorations, professional security, a professional DJ and sound equipment, and hors d'oeuvres—all to be selected by JoonBug but paid for by Guastavino's. I also asked for a 25 percent cut of the bar revenues, and for all the proceeds from tickets and at-the-door entry. Basically, I asked for the world!

The whole proposal was about four pages long and took me

about half a day to create. Looking back, I would describe it as a masterpiece of … BS. After all, I was asking for all this stuff on behalf of a made-up company that wasn't even incorporated, with a logo and website I'd thrown together just the day before. But I was truly convinced that Ariana and I could create a spectacular event, one that would make everyone involved a lot of money. All we needed was a green light.

It seemed to me that the best way to put things in motion would be to deliver the proposal in person, so I cold-called Guastavino's and asked for the manager. The receptionist transferred me to a pleasant but terse-sounding guy named Chris Malm.

"Hi Chris, this is Shane from JoonBug," I said casually, as if JoonBug were a household name. "We're considering Guastavino's for a very large event, and I'd like to come and meet with you to discuss it."

"Sure," Chris answered. "Will sometime later today work for you? I could also meet with you tomorrow." He threw out a few times that would work for him, and I decided to strike while the iron was hot, scheduling the meeting for that same afternoon. He agreed, and it was settled.

With just a couple of hours to prepare, I used the laser printer I had brought with me from Offyx to print two copies of the proposal. They looked terrific to me, and I slid them into a manila envelope with mounting excitement. Then I showered and put on one of my nice suits and a tie. Most of my good clothes at that time were black, suitable for formal events or evening wear, but luckily, I did have one navy-blue suit and a white button-down shirt. I put those on with a skinny navy tie, slicked my hair back with gel, and put on cologne—Drakkar Noir or Jean Paul Gaultier, which were the fashionable choices for men back then. Picking up the phone,

I called Ariana at work and tried to get her to come with me, but she was stuck and couldn't make it. So, five minutes before the meeting, I grabbed the manila envelope, walked to Guastavino's, and waited for Chris by the bar.

Let's Make a Deal

Chris walked out with another gentleman named Artan, who looked very European: long, thick, black hair, a linen suit with a fitted V-neck shirt underneath, and a long cotton shawl thrown around his neck. We shook hands, and each of them gave me his card. I didn't have any cards and tried to smooth that over by saying I had forgotten mine back at the office. Then I gestured to the manila envelope and said that they would find my information in the proposal.

They began to ask me about JoonBug and what we did, but I quickly deflected those questions, too. "Gentlemen, let's talk about that momentarily—I'm in a bit of a rush, so if you don't mind, can you please give me a tour of the venue? We can speak further afterwards if it fits my needs."

They agreed and took me around the whole place, showing me all its features and amenities. The more I saw, the more I could envision the Halloween party unfolding into a smashing success. If only I could convince them to book us! Over and over, my brain was telling me I *couldn't* screw this up, we *had* to work it out, we *had* to do the party, I *HAD* to book this venue!

But I continued to play it cool. After the tour, I thanked them both for showing me around. "I do think your space would be a good fit for our Halloween event. Here's a proposal for the night of the thirty-first. Please take some time to look it over, and let's talk again tomorrow. I have to move on to a meeting at another venue, and I'm running late."

They shook hands with me one more time and told me they'd review the proposal and get back to me first thing the next day. I didn't give them any time to ask further questions, as I didn't want them asking things I wasn't prepared to answer, and I wanted to give the impression that Guastavino's was just one out of several options JoonBug had on the table. Little did they know that they were my only option—and if they turned me down, it would be the beginning of the end of JoonBug, and another harsh reset to my life's trajectory!

By the time I got back to the apartment, Ariana was home from work. In a fever of excitement and nerves, I told her all about the meeting. I could see her slowly buying into the idea now that it was in motion. Up until then, although we were technically in agreement, she had remained somewhat skeptical. But now her excitement was growing, and neither of us could wait until the next day. In fact, I could hardly sleep that night. I kept turning the whole situation over and over in my mind, imagining what success would look like, and wondering what I would do if it didn't work out.

Late the next morning, I still hadn't gotten a call. It was agony to keep waiting, so I bit the bullet and called Chris. He admitted that they had reviewed the proposal, and that the night of Halloween was open for booking. But, he added, we needed to meet again. "Some details will have to be ironed out if you want to hold your event here."

That might not sound too encouraging, but all I could think was, "Bingo!"

Once I heard the part about ironing out the details, I knew that Guastavino's was in the bag. The devil might be in the details, but at least I was past the point of trying to fake my way into booking the venue. We set up a time later that day to go over the issues they had with my proposal, and I did the whole rigamarole again, putting on the suit, gelling my hair, adding cologne, yada yada yada.

When I got to Guastavino's, Chris, Artan, and I took our seats around one of the tables. As they laid out the terms of their counter-offer, I couldn't help but see a certain humor in the situation. Essentially, everything I had asked *them* to pay for, they now requested *me* to pay for: decorations, open bar, security, DJ, all of it. They also said that the most they'd give me from the bar revenue was ten percent. Finally, they asked for a $10,000 deposit up front, in case the event flopped! How the tables had turned.

But negotiating didn't bother me: I found it interesting. I knew we had to meet somewhere in the middle. It was just a matter of working out a good compromise.

Trying to think quickly and reasonably, I said JoonBug was willing to pay for the music and the decor, but that Guastavino's would have to provide an open bar. To sweeten the deal, I added that the open bar could be for just one hour, instead of two, and it could be at the beginning of the night, which is a slow time. I also said that Guastavino's would have to pay for security, and that JoonBug wanted 15 percent of the bar revenue.

The $10,000 deposit was the worst hurdle. I really had to think fast about that. My solution was to tell them they could hold my credit card; if there was a shortfall or discrepancy, they could charge it.

After I finished talking, we all looked at each other for about a minute. Then Chris said, "I think we can work that out."

I reached out and shook his hand, then Artan's, and told them I would send a revised proposal for execution later that day.

Find Me the Money

I walked home after that meeting with a giant smile on my face, but a terrible sinking feeling in my chest. Sure, I had closed the deal, but the things I had agreed to pay for were *way* out of reach financially.

Ariana and I were going to have to figure out some way to decorate an absolutely enormous event space without costing an arm and a leg, and at that moment, I had no idea how we would do it. In addition to decorations, I also had to find an amazing DJ. I had no clue how much that would cost, but if it were anything more than a few hundred bucks, we were in trouble. Most of all, I was worried that Chris might try to run my card before the party. Still, I moved forward, revised the proposal, including my credit card details this time, and left the rest to fate. Chris signed the proposal the next day, and then the real work began.

I knew that the only way to make money on this event was to create as much hype as possible. To do that, we needed to come up with marketing tactics no one had tried before. The first thing I did was update the JoonBug site, adding the party information along with the best pictures I could find of Guastavino's. Thankfully, they had used some of their millions to build an amazing website with beautiful photos I could copy.

Ariana and I threw around name ideas, and eventually came up with "Haunted Halloween Under the Vaulted Arches of the 59th Street Bridge." That was sure to pique everyone's interest. Who knew you could party under the famous bridge connecting Manhattan and Queens?

Next up were the physical invites. I definitely did not want a boring flyer, like the paper and cardboard ones always being dumped outside of clubs by flyer guys. I had seen way too many of those laying on the sidewalk and covered in shoe prints at four a.m.! What we needed was something different, something shiny and new that would grab attention and not be easily forgotten. In the end, ironically, I came up with the idea of giving out invitations that looked like credit cards.

I wanted them to not only look like credit cards, but *feel* like credit cards—embossed numbering, mag stripe, and all. Of course, the mag stripe wouldn't actually work or have any information on it, but that wasn't the point. No one else was doing anything even remotely like issuing credit cards as passports to their events, and it was exactly the kind of gimmick that would intrigue potential patrons.

After scouring the internet, I found a company in upstate New York that could make me exactly what I wanted. Their salesperson told me the cards would cost about twenty-five cents each, and they could make and ship them within a week.

I did the math. For 3,000 cards, it would be $750, which was … way too expensive. But by that point, I felt like I had to have them, whatever the cost. I decided to deal with the details later and asked the salesperson for the specs so that I could get the design ready.

It was again time to put my limited artistic skills to work. I started by putting the name of the party at the top, and then added the JoonBug logo, the Guastavino's logo, the address, and "By Invite Only." In the center, I put "Invite Code" followed by a string of random numbers to represent the embossed account number. Without really thinking, I also typed "Sponsored By."

I sat there for a second, looking at what I had just typed. Sponsored by? Again, bingo! Now I could see how to pay for the invites, the DJ, everything! We would get a company, or maybe even multiple companies, to sponsor our event! So obvious, and so easy—or at least, that's what I imagined, not realizing how hard it is to get sponsorship most of the time.

Back then, *TimeOut NY* was the only publication serving as a guide to New York City nightlife and restaurants. It seemed like the easiest thing to do would be to call the nightlife editor, tell her about our party, and see if she was interested in sponsoring us. In exchange, we could have their logo printed on the invites.

So, I picked up an issue of the magazine and checked the masthead for the nightlife editor's information. When I called, she answered on the second ring.

"Hi Amy," I said, in what I hoped sounded like a friendly but professional tone.

"Hi, who is this?" she asked.

I knew I had to be very matter-of-fact, just as I had been with Chris and Artan at Guastavino's. "Oh hey, this is Shane, from JoonBug. I was calling to speak to you about a sponsorship opportunity for a 3,000-plus Halloween party at Guastavino's under the 59th Street Bridge."

There was a pause. Clearly, she couldn't place me or my company, but she didn't necessarily want to admit that!

"Oh, yes, I've heard a little something about this event," she said casually. "What did you have in mind?"

Those words were music to my ears. Now I knew that she was the right person to talk to about sponsorship, and that our party was evidently the right size and type for *TimeOut NY* to sponsor.

"Well," I said, "We're making the invites right now, and they're going to be real, magnetic-stripe, plastic credit cards. I have room for your logo on the front of the cards, and on the event website as well."

No events that I knew of at that time had their own websites. This was before Facebook, before MySpace, even before evites. The internet had only recently become a viable communications medium, and we were the first to use it in the New York nightlife scene.

"If you give me your email, I can send you a copy of what the invite looks like and the website address. How does that sound?" Amy seemed genuinely excited, and readily gave me her email address. I hung up, on cloud nine. This was going to work, and it would solve all our problems! I could just imagine the whole night, sparkling like champagne: ritzy, intoxicating, and perfect. It would be a huge success.

I knew what I needed to do next: call Ariana and get a sponsorship proposal from The Miami Project. This time, since I already had the letterhead made, it was even quicker to make a JoonBug version. After that, I spent a few hours figuring out how to put the *TimeOut NY* logo onto my design for the credit cards, and a bit more time to update the JoonBug website.

When everything was all set, I read over the proposal one more time. I was asking for $2,000. In return, we would place the *TimeOut NY* logo on the invites as well as the website. I added that *TimeOut NY* could put up signage at the event and threw in ten complimentary tickets as well.

With the actual cost for the invitations being only $750, two grand was a lot to ask for. But in most cases, it's better to ask for more at first and negotiate a lower price later, if necessary. Rarely does a first offer get accepted, and it's important to take that into account; otherwise, you may end up negotiating down to make the deal, arriving at a number that doesn't really work for you.

On the other hand, if they did give me the full $2,000, I could order the invites and use the extra money for the DJ and decorations. I sent off the proposal, the credit-card mockup, and a link to the JoonBug website in an email late that afternoon. (That necessitated spending a little bit more time with my software-engineer hat on, because I needed a joonbug.com email address for myself, which wasn't as easy to do back then as it is now.)

The next morning, Amy sent back an email that read, "Thanks, Shane. I took a look, and it looks interesting. I'll try to see if we have a budget for this and get back to you."

Well, that was a buzzkill. From the way she had sounded on the phone the day before, I had assumed that the sponsorship would be a slam dunk. Slightly frazzled from the tension, and all the work I had put into making this happen, I waited, trying not to read too much into her words. But by the end of the day, she still hadn't gotten back in touch, and it was driving me freaking bonkers. I knew that my expectations were unrealistic, but I just had to have an answer.

The next day I gave her another call. This time, she recognized me, and we spent a few minutes exchanging polite banter. Then I cut to the chase.

"Amy, listen, I don't want to pressure you or anything. But my boss is telling me to reach out to a few more sponsors and get this wrapped up." Was that true? I guess, since I was my own boss, and I really needed to find a sponsor as soon as possible, it was *sort of* true. I kept on, persistently faking it.

"I think this is going to be a perfect opportunity for you, and from our conversation yesterday, I think it's something you want to do. That said, is there any way you can get an answer from your side, perhaps today, so I can tell my boss we're committed?" Please, just let me tell my "boss" we're committed, I thought.

To my surprise, she took this all very understandingly, and agreed to talk to her boss that morning and get back to me with an answer by the end of the day. Now that was more like it! My confidence skyrocketed again.

But nothing is that simple, right? Around four o'clock that afternoon, I got an email back from Amy with good news and bad news.

The good news was that *TimeOut NY* wanted to move forward with the sponsorship. The bad news was that the most they could pay was $1,000.

This put me in a hard spot. Accepting this offer would basically show that the invites cost a lot less than the two grand I had requested, which didn't make me look too good. And accepting a counterproposal that was only half of my original offer? Not the direction I wanted to go, especially if we were going to work together again in the future. It would give them the impression I didn't want to make that they could heavily undercut my offers.

I let things marinate for a while, trying to figure out a way to make it work. Nothing seemed right until I came up with the idea of a co-sponsorship. I would tell Amy that we could work things out if she was willing to be a co-sponsor with another company, sharing the logo space and other benefits. I could also take advantage of her insight and contacts to find the other sponsor, by asking if she worked with any liquor companies that might be interested.

That's what I did, and amazingly, it worked! Amy told me that she had been working with Bacardi quite a bit, and that they had a large budget for this exact type of event. With the Bacardi logo being a black bat, our Halloween party would fit their brand perfectly, and vice versa. She put me in touch with Brian Axelrod, who handled all sponsorships and branding for Bacardi at that time, and Brian and I eventually settled on a $2,000 sponsorship.

This brought the sponsorship funds to three grand, which was much more than I had anticipated! I worked things out with Guastavino's so that, during the open bar, they would only serve Bacardi drinks. They agreed willingly when they realized that Bacardi would supply all the bottles during that hour!

Everything was covered: invites, decorations, a DJ whom Ariana chose—since she knew most of them, and her taste in music was admittedly much better than mine. The invites arrived on time in two long boxes. It was truly magical to open them and reveal the long rows of perfect, shiny credit cards inside. Anyone who received one would definitely be intrigued!

I was sure that people would feel compelled to check out the website—and once they did, if they wanted to accept the invitation, they'd have to put in their "Invite Code" and contact data, including their name, email, and phone number. That was part of JoonBug's payoff.

I had programmed all this, of course. It wasn't very difficult, after all the advanced programming I had worked on for Offyx. Basically, the system would insert the user's Invite Code and info into a database, and then send a sleek-looking confirmation email in return, with the event details, logos, and somewhere down at the bottom in teeny-tiny letters, the $30 admission price.

Finally, I decided to make a second email invitation to send out to personal contacts that Ariana and I had email addresses for. This was also novel at the time. Nice-looking email invitations just weren't being done, and on top of that, it was a bit tricky to write a program that would generate a unique Invite Code for each email sent. But we did it, and the response rate went through the roof.

Pounding the Pavement

All of that was digital work, and the real physical work was yet to come. Ariana and I now had to get the invites into the hands of the right partygoers in NYC. To do so, we made a pact to go out at least six nights a week, for as many weeks as it took, hitting as many different parties and clubs as we could.

Basically, we were poaching the events' patrons from within, but no one was the wiser! For about four weeks straight, we persistently worked the clubs, taking fifty to seventy-five invites with us each night and giving them out to everyone we ran into. Ariana naturally had the best luck with groups of guys, while I usually handed out cards to groups of girls. By the end of those four weeks, we were all out of cards, and the RSVP database had amassed over 5,000 recipients.

It was absolutely incredible … and terrifying. What would we do if over 5,000 people actually showed up? I couldn't imagine. We weren't prepared for a party on that scale. This worried me a lot, and I wondered if this was going to be one of those cases where you're too successful for your own good.

Ariana helpfully pointed out that only about 60 to 70 percent of the people who RSVP actually come to a given event, which was something of a relief. Still, we knew that there would also be plenty of attendees who *didn't* RSVP: friends of friends, and partiers who would decide at the last minute to come and check things out. That could mean a significant boost in the number of people at the party.

It also meant that there was still more data to be had. And the way I saw it, the more data we had, the higher our chances of future success would be. I tried to think of a gimmick that would allow us to collect data from the non-RSVP crowd. It needed to be something viral, something that would demand people's attention and pique their curiosity.

That's when I thought of getting a camera and hiring a photographer for the night to go around taking photos of the party. I could post the photos on our website for everyone to see. After all, it's only natural for people to want to see pictures of themselves, especially having a blast at an amazing party. And photography at nightclubs wasn't really happening at the time, especially not for regular parties—maybe special celebrity or brand events, but that was all.

Now that cell phone cameras are so sophisticated, it might seem odd to hire a photographer for that purpose. Selfies are all the rage, and everyone knows how to take their own pictures and publish them instantly on social media. But back then, camera phones were janky, maybe one megapixel at most, and clunky to use. Plus, getting pictures off a Motorola and onto a computer was almost impossible. The age of Instagram was still far in the future.

Digital cameras, on the other hand, were good, although new and super-expensive. I really wanted to use one, but the little bit of extra money in my budget didn't cover the purchase price.

Therefore, my next stop was the famous electronics store in Union Square called "The Wiz." I found the latest model digital camera and bought it using my credit card, while planning to return it the next day: The Wiz had a generous, thirty-day refund policy. Then I put out an ad on craigslist for a photographer and got fifty responses within an hour! After sifting through about fifteen of them, I found a guy who was willing to do it for just fifty bucks and a free ticket to the party.

But this great idea came with its own set of complications. People knew they should RSVP, because the invites told them to. That made getting their data simple. But how would our guests know that they should check JoonBug.com to see their photos? We would have to tell them somehow.

The easiest way that I could think of was to give them something similar to the credit card invites with the details printed on it. In the end, I settled on business cards, which could be printed cheaply and quickly, handed out, and stowed away in pockets or purses. Bingo.

It was time for me to sharpen my design skills one more time.

I made a simple business card layout with big bold type that said, "You've Been Bitten by the" and then, underneath that, the JoonBug logo. At the bottom, it read, "See your pictures at www.JoonBug. com." As a final touch, I made the card's background red, so that it would stand out.

I knew a printer in the city by the name of Roee, a regular on the nightlife scene, who had done flyers on the cheap for some of my friends. I was able to work out a deal with him to print 5,000 of the cards for the amazingly low price of $250, with a few comp tickets thrown in. Best of all, he agreed to let me pay him *after* the party! I emailed him my design, and two days later, I had the beautiful red cards in my possession.

Lights, Camera...

With one day left to go before Halloween, everything we'd worked to accomplish was coming together, and it was time to meet with all the people who'd be working for us that night. We all gathered at Guastavino's: Ariana and me, the staff and security, the DJ, and the sponsors. Ariana took the reins to direct the logistics of how the night should go.

Step by step, she laid out how the door line would work, where the security should be, what music the DJ would play at what time, and how the decorations should look. She knew what would be out on the bar, and what specific drinks would be served during the open bar portion of the evening. She also handled the sponsors like a pro, getting them to change requests that wouldn't have made much sense or would have been too difficult to implement, including the Bacardi sponsor's idea to hang a huge Bacardi bat from the seventy-five-foot vaulted ceiling.

My only task that night was to focus on the photographer. I'd invited him to come to the meeting and do a walk-through, so we spent about twenty minutes walking and talking, discussing the kind of photos he should be looking for. But the main thing I wanted him to understand was the importance of our JoonBug business cards. I basically told him that his objective was to take as many photos of as many people as possible, and to give each person in the photos a card. If he took multiple pictures of the same people over the course of the evening, he was to give them multiple cards.

I said that if he could take enough pictures and hand out all the cards, I would have a nice bonus for him at the end of the party. That's when his eyes lit up, and he gave me a nod that let me know he would pull out all the stops, going on a photo-taking spree and passing out cards to everyone. That was perfect. I knew that if we played our cards right, we could potentially double our database. JoonBug could go viral!

...Action!

On the day of the event, Ariana was as cool as a cucumber. Overseeing the staff and supplies and everything else was business as usual for her. But for me, it was overwhelming. I continually analyzed and re-analyzed every detail, sweating the small stuff, and mostly just worried instead of being productive.

We arrived at Guastavino's a few hours early, helped set up, and did one final walkthrough. Then we had a brief meeting with security about the doors, discussing how the ropes should be placed, how the lines should form, and how to process the guests. It was actually a great situation; the street in front of Guastavino's isn't typically crowded, and there were two access points in the massive entrance. We could form two lines and make the whole thing more efficient. We placed the cashier stands between the two sets of double doors and positioned security guards accordingly.

By then, it was about 7:30 p.m. The doors wouldn't open until 8 p.m., but when I glanced outside, there was already a line forming. That got my blood pumping. The weather was good too—maybe a little cold, but definitely bearable even for costume-wearers without jackets. That meant more people would come out.

At 8 p.m., the line was long enough to wrap around the corner. A feeling of apprehension began to creep over me. How were we going to process all these people? We had instructed them to either print their email confirmation or bring their card invites to swipe (which didn't actually work, but still). As the line grew, so did my anxiety. I realized that, with literally thousands of people expected to show up, it would take hours to check all their IDs, collect all their payments—in cash, no less; there wasn't any easy, portable way of taking credit cards, looking at their email confirmation numbers or swiping their invite cards back then.

"It's not going to work. What are we going to do? This is gonna take hours," I whispered to Ariana. She glanced at the line.

"Shane, calm down. It's going to be fine. Everyone will get in," she said. But I couldn't let go of my anxiety. Eventually she added, "If you stand here and worry, everyone else around you will worry too. They'll think something is wrong and feed off that vibe! Just chill. If you act like nothing's wrong, then everything will work itself out."

Once Ariana said that, I snapped out of it. With my anxiety at bay, I was able to think more clearly, and I suddenly realized that it didn't make sense to check everyone's invite. It was dark, things were taking too much time, and ultimately it didn't freaking matter because we were going to let everyone in, anyway! I told everyone to stop checking the invites, and the line started moving faster.

Then I noticed that everyone who got to the door was digging through their pockets or purses to get their IDs out, so I asked one of the security guys to go up and down the line and tell everyone to have their IDs ready. That sped things up even more. At one point, I jumped behind the cashier's desk and checked people in myself. I was faking it until I made it, in real time!

By 10 p.m., Guastavino's was packed with at least 3,000 people. Another line was forming, but we had to hold the door due to capacity issues, only letting in more patrons as others trickled out. The music was on point, the lights were going off, and happy partygoers decked out in amazing costumes were drinking and dancing everywhere, having a blast. Best of all, the photographer was circling through the crowds the whole night. People were actually stopping him and asking him to take their pictures, especially the girls who had gone all out getting dressed up. I saw red JoonBug cards littering the floor, but that was good news; it was proof that my photographer was handing them out like I'd asked him to!

Running the Numbers

We started to clean up at around 4 a.m., after all of our guests had left. I should have felt exhausted. Instead, I was amped up and clear-minded, as if I had just woken up from a full night's sleep. Ariana walked around with the staff and sponsors, wrapping up the logistical stuff. I took care of reconciling and securing the cash from the cashiers.

We had a clicker that security would use each time someone walked into the venue, and it showed that 4,900 people had come to the party. That was incredible. I couldn't wait to count the money we had collected! But that wasn't the time or the place, obviously, so I took the cash boxes, invites, cards, and other stuff and shoved it all into my locking briefcase leftover from Offyx. Before locking it, I counted out payments and tips for the cashiers, security guards, DJ, and most importantly, the photographer. He gave me back the camera, and I checked the memory card. It was filled to capacity, with more than 2,500 photos of the night. That warranted a fat bonus. He was super happy, but I think I was happier!

When Ariana and I were finally finished with all of the wrapping-up, we asked one of the security guards to walk us home, since it was only a couple of blocks away, and we were carrying the cash. Once we got inside, the excitement really started.

I opened up the briefcase and stopped in my tracks. Back at Guastavino's, I had been in such a rush that I hadn't realized quite how much money I was handling. Now, in the light, seeing all that cash was absolutely exhilarating. Ariana and I looked at each other, started laughing, and put in about an hour of sorting, stacking, and counting. Our energy was renewed, and we couldn't believe what we were doing.

The grand total was $109,000. Accounting for the two grand we'd started with, and the $3,000 or so we'd handed out for tips and payments, we had made about $110,000 in the span of eight hours.

Taking Stock and Making Strides

All those weeks of faking, improvising, and dreaming had paid off, big time. The money we were looking at didn't even include our cut of the bar revenues, and at that point we didn't care: it would just be gravy.

In no time, we were feverishly brainstorming ideas for our next party: what we could do, how we could pull it off, and how if we just did one party like this each month, we would be bringing in over a million dollars a year. We'd become millionaires, just throwing parties! My dreams (and mental to-do list) were getting bigger and more grandiose by the second.

I couldn't sleep after all of that. Instead, I got to work down-loading all the photos to my computer so that I could upload them to JoonBug.com. It took hours; both cameras and PCs were a lot slower than they are now. There was barely enough disk space on my computer to hold them all! And once they were downloaded, I had to figure out how to get them onto the website in the way I had envisioned. I wanted a nice gallery design, but it had to be coded from scratch. No easy, shortcut website builders like Wix and Squarespace were around back then.

It would be way too crazy and time-consuming to manually create the pages in HTML and hand-code the images in. So instead, I worked through the morning and into the afternoon writing a program that would process the images and create the HTML needed for the gallery to reference them. It functioned pretty well on the test run, and after working out the bugs, I had a professional-looking photo gallery. Then came more hours of coding, this time to make a data wall to block users from accessing the photos unless they registered with our site. All their data would be funneled into the RSVP database, which by that time had grown to over 7,000 subscribers.

Meanwhile, I had totally forgotten my plan to return the camera to The Wiz. When I did remember, all I could think was that not only did we need the camera for our next event, but we probably needed two of them!

At 7 p.m., the evening after the party, I posted the photos and the registration system, crashed into bed, and slept for a few hours. It was around 1 a.m. when I woke up, staggered to the bathroom, and then headed back to bed. But on the way, I decided to quickly fire up my computer for a second to see if anyone had registered to see their photos.

I rubbed my eyes. Was I seeing this right? The site had received over a thousand registered users, just in the few hours I'd been sleeping. And every time I refreshed the database, there were more! Entranced, I kept refreshing and refreshing and refreshing the database. Watching the number grow was like getting a hit of crack every time!

After half an hour, the website crashed. I scrambled to figure out what was going on. It turned out there were just too many people visiting the site at once, and the server couldn't handle that much traffic. I had to whip out my credit card and upgrade our web hosting plan to a larger server. Within an hour, we were up and running again—only to crash again shortly thereafter. I bought another upgrade, and another. This went on for about a week, and when all was said and done, we hit 35,000 subscribers.

Clearly, we were on to something amazing. I made up my mind completely: JoonBug would become my life, and I was going to turn it into the biggest online media and events company in Manhattan. After all, I was now armed with what was arguably the largest database of young, urban professionals in the city, all of whom had disposable income and an interest in nightlife. I had dangerous-enough computer skills to build advanced websites that could rival many of the big boys out there, and I had a partner who could execute spectacular events in her sleep. Lastly, we had sponsors who loved us and loads of money to spend! Our recipe for success was clear, and we had all the ingredients. It was time to get cooking!

Nightlife Lessons Learned

The roller-coaster ride of throwing my first big party taught me two related lessons: *Persistence Beats Resistance* and *Fake It Till You Make It.*

It's hard not to be distraught when you're unknown and first starting out. You call, email, and text people, not knowing if anyone will actually show up. No one gives you the respect you want. You're only as good as your last event, but if you're just starting out, you don't even have a last event to be judged by!

The possibility of failure is real and sometimes high. Every promoter and club owner I know has gone through major periods of failure. And there's no doubt that planning a big bash and renting a place, just to have it all flop, is emotionally defeating (and can be financially disastrous).

In these circumstances, the people who win are the ones who have the emotional fortitude to withstand failure and rejection and keep moving forward anyway. Persistence beats resistance.

In a similar vein, success often requires faking it 'til you make it. You're going to have to bullshit people and pretend that you're bigger and better than you are, so that they actually pay attention to you. And that may take a very long time!

These two lessons are so interrelated that they are almost one and the same. You have to fake it long and persistently enough that everybody starts to believe it and then, through a lot of hard work and a little magic, it becomes real.

These lessons have served me well in my subsequent ventures. When I started EZ Texting, I had never had a successful software company before. Just one that had folded in the dot-com crash. Without a prior success story to point back to, we had to come up with a way to hook our leads with a few sentences. The ones that worked (after trying hundreds of variations) were: "Hey, we have a way to automatically collect the cell phone numbers of everybody who comes into your store (or club, or restaurant, or whatever). Then you can text them the next day, or the next week, and tell them if a sale or an event is going on."

Was that true? Well, not exactly. It was a quick and very simplified summary. But in the minds of the people we were pitching to, it was extremely appealing. It got them on the hook, enough for them to agree to sign up for a demo. Once we booked them on a demo, we would almost always close the sale. Yes, the process was a little more complicated than it first appeared, but the service delivered what the customers wanted.

Although I'm no longer very involved, EZ Texting remains a big business with hundreds of thousands of customers. And the one-sentence marketing hook funneling to a demo technique is one I've used successfully in many projects since and have also suggested it to the startup founders I invest in.

Essentially, faking it 'til you make it is not only a legitimate way of breaking into a new business (provided that you can deliver on your promises), it's often the *only* way of breaking in when you don't have a track record. So be fake—and while you're at it, be persistent!

LESSON 2

EXCLUSIVITY DOESN'T PAY THE BILLS

"NOT TONIGHT, BRO." THIS WAS the line that the legendary NYC doorman Wass Stevens used for years to turn people away from exclusive clubs such as Veruka and Avenue. Eventually, it became such a well-known catchphrase that he turned it into a brand.

Exclusivity is a big thing in nightlife. Some of the most popular clubs in NYC history centered their business model on exclusivity: Bungalow 8, Socialista, Pangaea, PM, Lot 61, and Cain, just to name a few. The idea is to craft an experience that is meant only for the elite. If that succeeds, then celebrities, models, and other VIPs will flock to the club. Those people usually get comped, of course, but they're followed by tons of wealthy wannabes who are willing to shell out big bucks to be part of the in-crowd.

Ultimately, though, exclusivity is a strategy that's destined to fail.

At first, it might seem awesome to be the coolest, most exclusive place in town, but as time goes by, the only way to make money is by growing and expanding your business. Exclusivity makes that difficult, if not impossible, because by definition it means turning down big crowds, walking away from big brands, and missing out on big opportunities. The moral of this story? You need more than trendiness to build a lasting brand.

Trendsetting (At First)

Most of the ultra-exclusive places that open up, even successfully, nevertheless wind up closing in short order. The reason? Their business model isn't built with long-term gains in mind but instead is driven by ego. Most owners believe that their spot will last forever—that somehow, *this* time it's going to be different. The usual recipe for these clubs is to open with a big PR campaign, spending a ton of money comping celebrities, press, socialites, and models, in order to create a big buzz. This is meant to help the fledgling club attract the attention of New York City trendsetters and gossip magazines. By the end of the first month, if all goes well, the buzz pays off, and crowds start to gather.

But the club owners must continue turning almost everyone away to maintain their reputation as "exclusive." Aside from people too cool and too beautiful to charge, owners and promoters can only let in a few ultra-rich Wall Street types, guys who are willing to pay to play. The pay-to-play patrons are the ones owners are counting on, money-wise, because they purchase bottle-service tables. These guys sometimes drop tens of thousands of dollars in a single night, just to hang out with the (non-paying) celebrity crowd!

Within about six months, however, most of the celebrities and socialites are already becoming disenchanted with the club, flitting off to the next up-and-coming hotspot. At that point, the club typically transitions from VIP-only to a 50/50 mix of ordinary patrons and "cool crowd." Within a year, formerly exclusive clubs often go totally mainstream, catering mostly to the bridge-and tunnel crowd, and doing ethnic or urban nights with promoters who specialize in those niches.

A Losing Proposition

Interestingly, while losing VIP clientele might sound like a bad thing, in reality, that's when clubs are poised to make the *maximum* amount of money. They're still attracting large crowds, but now (almost) everyone is paying. It's a much simpler and more lucrative situation than trying to attract a handful of wealthy patrons to go on massive spending sprees.

But here's the catch. Most of the places considered ultra-hotspots are also quite small. This is a deliberate design choice, because if these venues were huge, it would be difficult to fill them up with VIPs. However, when your venue is small, and you can only let in so many people, then you can only charge so many patrons. Therefore, you can only make so much money. You're capped.

By this point in the club's lifecycle, the owner is usually swamped in debt, not paying rent, and desperate to bring in some kind of profit before the venue's inevitable closure. And since these types of owners aren't in it to build a sustainable business anyway, they do what comes naturally to small-minded, money-hungry people: they default, keep the money, and leave everyone else in the dust.

It was usually during the second, 50/50 phase that club owners and promoters would approach JoonBug for advertising, email blasts, photography, and other services. In the beginning, at the height of their popularity with the trendsetting crowd, they would snub us, saying we were too mainstream. But we always knew they'd change their tune once the buzz receded, paying us, and sometimes even pleading with us, to fill up their venues. It was a vicious, yet predictable, cycle.

JoonBug and the Whale

Early on, JoonBug started offering a VIP concierge service to cater to the more exclusive, upscale clubs and patrons. We called it JoonBug Elite. I even designed a special mini-website just for JoonBug Elite, and Ariana and I ran it personally.

In those days, customer relationship management systems like Salesforce didn't exist—so I created a custom CRM of our own. Basically, it was a database of our elite contacts, whom we had vetted, and with whom we had personal relationships. We tracked where they liked to party, how much they spent (that is, if they weren't celebs and models getting comped), what they looked like, and what kind of music they preferred. Then we slotted them into the system, using categories such as "Model," "Celebrity," "Media," "PR," "Wall Street," and "Whale."

Whales were the most sought-after clients a club could have—the few-and-far-between mega-spenders who would drop upward of fifty grand in one night (that's equal to about seventy-five grand adjusted for inflation in 2023). A whale would think nothing of buying the most expensive bottle service, and on top of that, spontaneously springing for extra bottles left and right: for their own table, the table next to them, and even the whole club!

The Frank Phenomenon

JoonBug had relationships with a few of them, but there was one in particular who was a truly giant whale. His name was Frank Fazzio—or that's what he told us his name was, anyway.

Ariana and I first met him when Guastavino's hired JoonBug to promote a regular Saturday night event there. After our initial Halloween party, Chris and Artan had practically begged us to take a weekend night for them and promote it on a weekly basis. At first, we were hesitant. Would we be able to consistently bring in large crowds, week after week?

On the other hand, we did have a large database from Halloween, and it was still growing like crazy. Plus, Guastavino's was willing to give us all the money collected at the door and 25 percent of the bar's gross sales. That was a huge chunk of money! So, we decided to give it a shot.

Frank showed up on one of the first Saturday nights we did there and brought along a few friends. Our doorman, an off-duty cop named Jimmy, came and asked us if we wanted to let them in. I was hesitant at first; we were being picky in the initial stages, and I wasn't sure about these guys, even if they bought a table.

"Tell him it's a $10,000 minimum," I said finally. Jimmy nodded and headed back to the ropes. Then something crazy happened. Jimmy walked right back in, leading Frank and his crew of meathead pals to the bar where Ariana and I were seated. Obviously, this Frank guy had agreed to my outrageous price tag on the spot.

But Jimmy didn't just bring them to the bar; he came right up to me so that he could lean in and speak confidentially. Frank, he whispered, had actually agreed to a $15,000 minimum.

I was stunned. Quickly, we sprang into action, rolling out the proverbial red carpet. Jimmy radioed Artan to explain the situation, and Artan hurried in a moment later, flanked by scantily clad bottle-service girls, to prepare the center table on the second floor for Frank and his crew. Ariana, Jimmy, and I escorted them up there; it was the best table in the house, with the best view of all the action.

Ariana and I sat down with Frank, making small talk and getting acquainted. Frank said that he was a construction contractor with a vinyl-siding business, and I told him a bit about what we did at JoonBug. We exchanged phone numbers, and I told him to call me personally anytime he wanted to come to Guastavino's or anywhere else in the city.

Then Ariana and I got up to leave, but as we did, Frank grabbed my arm. I looked down at him, and his eyes held mine in a sober, inscrutable gaze. In his thick, New York-Italian accent, he told me, "I like youse guys. An' I can tell I can trust youse guys. Youse good people."

I think it was at that moment I realized that Frank might not be just a contractor with a vinyl-siding business. But I didn't want to know, and it was none of my business anyway. As long as he would come to our parties, be happy, and spend a ton of money, it didn't really matter to me what he did!

Just then, the DJ switched the music to the Superman theme, and five pretty bottle-service girls came marching in formation to Frank's table, holding two huge magnums of Grey Goose and Kristal, each with Fourth-of-July sparklers on top. They lit the sparklers and danced around, creating a spectacle that drew every eye to Frank's table. Once the music had quieted down and the sparklers had faded, the girls got started pouring drinks for everyone.

Within seconds, women from all over the club were flocking around Frank and his friends, accepting free drinks, and flirting outrageously. The guys were absolutely dripping with girls and having the time of their lives. Frank was enjoying himself tremendously and kept offering me and Ariana drinks as well. We didn't refuse, but we also didn't partake. We just took pretend sips and then set our glasses down on the table to be lost among the rest.

Frank in Full Force

From that night on, Frank was glued to JoonBug, calling us all the time. While we also made friends with other regulars who bought bottles from us, Frank was by far the biggest whale of them all, and in a class of his own when it came to contacting us.

He was from Howard Beach, a notorious Italian neighborhood that was once home to John Gotti. It got to the point where he was inviting us to dinner at his favorite neighborhood restaurant on a regular basis. We were becoming a part of his posse (and I was gaining weight) with every plate of veal parmigiana.

In fact, keeping up with JoonBug while also keeping up with Frank started to become harder and harder. He and the other JoonBug Elite patrons blew up our phones at all hours of the day and night, and they had no shortage of demands. Eventually, we found ourselves scrambling to get them not only into JoonBug's events, but also into other clubs and parties that had nothing to do with us. Somehow, we had morphed from being the founders of JoonBug to being Frank's and the Elites' on-call, personal party concierges.

Fuhgeddaboudit!

The time-suck of catering to Frank and the others was amusing at first, but eventually Ariana and I realized that it didn't make good business sense. We did an analysis, and although the money we were making from them was good, it didn't even come close to justifying the time and energy we were putting in. It turned out that our Elite clients represented less than 20 percent of our revenue but consumed almost 80 percent of our time—the converse of the famous 80/20 rule!

We decided to just stick with the masses. After almost a year of trying to make JoonBug Elite work and spending a lot of money and time building out the custom website and CRM from scratch, we finally made up our minds and sunsetted the whole thing. It had been a good run, but it just wasn't scalable, and frankly, ending it was a big relief. Being at someone else's beck and call all the time had really sucked—it's the unglamorous side of being a promoter that outsiders don't really see.

It took about a month for the constant calls to finally stop, but eventually, everyone who was used to having us on speed dial accepted that we were done, and presumably moved on. That gave me tons more time to focus on our business, in particular the technology stack, the big events that were growing our list of customers, and most importantly, our database.

Nightlife Lessons Learned

While you might want to start with exclusivity, it doesn't pay the bills and won't make you rich. It might feel awesome to be the coolest and most exclusive place in town, but ultimately, the only way to make money is to grow and expand. If you're too exclusive, you have to turn down large crowds, big brands, and everything else that comes with making big money.

Look at some of the most successful nightlife entrepreneurs, such as Noah Tepperberg and Jason Strauss of TAO Group, Richie Akiva and Scott Sartiano of Butter Group, and Eugene Remm and Mark Birnbaum of Catch Hospitality Group. They went from having tough doors and places you couldn't get into to building global brands out of their most successful venues.

It's just a simple fact. You can't build a business solely around a base of celebrity clients who are too cool to pay. Someone has to pay, or no one gets paid! But if you accept that you need to cater to a large number of ordinary patrons, you can build a sustainable business that not only survives but grows. And the bigger you get, the more money you'll make, with less effort. The network effects of having tons of subscribers and a growing base of customers can't be beat.

That's how it works for hotspots, and that's how it worked for JoonBug. The money is in the masses, and that's who we focused on, moving forward. Promoters seeking fame, status, and getting laid could go on chasing their tails and their high-end clientele. We were better off serving the people who didn't even know our names, but followed our brand instead, and paid us for the privilege.

In a similar vein, when I first started EZ Texting, we called it Club Texting. But shortly after that, I realized that I was pigeonholing the venture with that name. I didn't want people thinking that it was a service exclusively for clubs. Yes, our first customers were people we already knew from the nightlife scene, but our service wasn't just for them. So, I changed the name to expand our total addressable market. That helped me land many different kinds of customers and caused business to boom.

Now, as a venture capitalist, I often see the same elitism with startups. You have to know the right people to get into the right VCs to invest. Even if you're smart and have a good idea for a startup, it's still really hard to get in front of a successful VC firm if you don't know someone who knows someone there. After all, these firms get thousands of submissions, so they put on automatic filters, and the first one is usually "who do they know that I know?"

Another thing that most VCs consider is whether or not someone has previously founded, and successfully exited, a venture. Successful multi-exit founders are a rare breed, coveted by VCs as part of an elite club.

However, I always try to give anyone who comes to me at least some of my time. I don't look at the "pedigree" of the founder or try to figure out who they know that I know. The truth is that just because a person moves in certain circles or had success in the past doesn't mean they're going to be successful this time around. The chances of success may be higher, but they're far from guaranteed. And there are a *lot* of lucrative opportunities out there that get overlooked, due to this restrictive mindset. Exclusivity doesn't pay the bills!

YOU'RE SELLING A FEELING... SO MAKE IT A GOOD ONE

HAVE YOU EVER BEEN IN a nightclub when the lights are on? It's not pretty. But in nightlife, you're not selling a product: you're selling a feeling. Glamour, intrigue, buzz, and chaos are what motivate patrons to flock to a club, even if it's a dump. Which, as a matter of fact, popular clubs often are. Some of the most profitable hotspots in NYC history have been little more than lightly decorated disasters in seedy locations.

The same goes for nightlife professionals. You might think that presenting yourself as sophisticated and attracting "beautiful people" to your club could make or break a club's reputation, which in turn could make or break your career. Right?

Well, yes and no. While some promoters definitely leveraged their looks to further their careers, others did nothing of the sort.

To be a successful promoter and strategist, looks don't matter at all. What does matter is having charisma, paying attention to detail, and making people feel like a million bucks. Figure that out, and everyone will swipe their cards.

Does this translate across industries? You bet—from JoonBug and EZ Texting to my work as a venture capitalist, selling a feeling has been key to building a successful business.

Best Sellers

Back in the day, nightclubs opened up in all kinds of bizarre locations: warehouses, basements, and other odd, out-of-the-way places that people wouldn't normally want to visit. The obvious bonus for doing this was that it would provoke curiosity and maybe a little excitement—especially important in a time when most people found out about new clubs via word of mouth.

But on top of that, there were plenty of strategic advantages to these areas. For one thing, in an industry as fickle as nightlife, owners needed to find spaces cheap enough for them to turn a profit and leases they could easily break if the club went under. Lack of oversight was a plus, as well. It made getting a liquor license and approval from the local community board a lot easier than it would have been in fancier, more gentrified parts of NYC.

So, club after club opened and closed in venues that ranged from seedy to downright dilapidated. And like magic, dazzling crowds of glitterati lined up behind velvet ropes, hoping to get inside and feel the pulse of New York City itself. That juxtaposition—abandoned cityscapes, coveted cachet, trashy surroundings, hot music, and liquor—created a feeling that passionate party-seekers couldn't resist.

As I look back, there are a few clubs that really stand out in this category. They excelled at selling a feeling, regardless of how they looked in the cold light of day.

PM

PM, a club that opened in the Manhattan Meatpacking District, was a perfect example. The Meatpacking District was exactly what it sounds like. Once home to hundreds of slaughterhouses and meat wholesalers, it had been going downhill for decades by the time PM came along, but even then, it was still a bustle of meat businesses moving meat in and out of warehouses. During the day, customers in search of wholesale prices braved the terrible stench to pick their way around puddles of blood, animal fat, and offal. At night, those crowds gave way to sex workers who haunted the deserted streets, catering to their own clientele.

But Haitian brothers Unik and Kyky Ernest introduced a whole new dynamic to that area. They found a building there with lofty ceilings and old-school architecture and used it to open PM, a nightclub lounge that immediately became one of the most coveted places to see and be seen in all of NYC. Thanks to PM, the entire shabby, obscure district would eventually transform into one of NYC's trendiest areas, attracting couturiers, luxury hotels, five-star restaurants, art galleries, and of course, more nightclubs.

PM itself was super small, holding maybe 150 people at most. For ambience and decor, the Ernest brothers put in some couches, added a makeshift bar, and had a few 1980s-style glass brick walls arranged around the space. Exposed ceiling rafters and some decorative items here and there completed the physical makeup of this ultra-popular hotspot. If that doesn't sound like much … well, it wasn't.

But hordes of wannabes, models, sugar daddies, and the rest lined up outside for a chance to get in. They devoured spicy plates of tapas, downed colorful Haitian cocktails, danced, and soaked up the magic, because say what you like about the physical surroundings, Unik Ernest was a celebrity darling with a history of throwing amazing parties at the city's best hotspots. He knew how to sell a feeling, and where he led, A-listers followed—even (and maybe especially) if it meant jumping over huge puddles of filth on cobblestone streets to get there.

Pangaea

Pangaea, too, had the magic. Located near the NYU and Cooper Union campus, in an area that had been mostly overlooked until then, the building itself was a nondescript, 4,000-square-foot rectangle with one huge door.

But Michael Ault hung an antelope head with long, protruding horns on that door—and somehow immediately set it apart as something unexpected, and maybe a little bit dangerous.

Inside, there was not much more than a bar, a few tribal masks, some (supposedly authentic) African beads, and about twenty "tables" that were just glorified couch banquettes covered in fake animal skins. No dance floor, no fancy sound system, no nothing.

Despite this, for about five years, Pangaea was by far the coolest nightclub in NYC. It was my generation's Studio 54: an iconic venue that epitomized the glitzy, gritty, beautiful, and bizarre world of nightlife in the '90s.

Pangaea's whole vibe centered around the exotic. The effect has been described as "tribal fantasy" and really, that was how it felt. It didn't matter that the decor was simplistic or even fake. It felt like something from another world, and everyone tried to get in. For those who did, the feeling of fantasy and adventure was utterly intoxicating.

GoldBar

Finally, there was GoldBar.

Opened by Jamie Mulholland and designed by Rob McKinley, GoldBar held maybe fifty people at a time, with only a handful of tables seating five patrons each. Jamie had set his sights on a location that rubbed elbows with Chinatown and had never been home to anything like a nightclub before—no one had ever thought to build one there! GoldBar opened in a decrepit little building with nothing but an empty parking lot nearby.

To make the place stand out, Rob and Jamie came up with arguably one of the cheesiest schemes ever, at least on the face of it. What they did was use cheap plastic skulls, painted gold, to line the walls. Then they concocted a goofy backstory about an Italian count who was so obsessed with gold that he created this golden-skulled cavern, living there until his death. To finish the look, they hung flea-market paintings as "portraits" of the count and his family, added some curtains and plenty of gold paint, and purposely graffitied the bathrooms instead of renovating them.

Looking back, it was all so silly. But for patrons partying in the dark (most of them with vodka goggles on), it felt like a dream. With gold flecks in the cocktails, beautiful models lounging and dancing, irresistible music, and not quite enough room on a breathless summer night, it was a feeling that the glitterati couldn't resist. For years, GoldBar attracted the cream of the nightlife crowd. It was the Cartier of nightclubs.

A Swing and a Miss

On the opposite end of the spectrum, I can recall a number of nightclubs that cost tons of money to build out but failed to evoke the right feelings in patrons (or any feelings at all). Even though the owners spared no expense to make their venues look as beautiful and "designer" as possible, it was all for nil. Two of those clunkers stand out in my mind.

Duvet

Duvet was a gimmicky place on 21st Street in Chelsea, right next door to our JoonBug offices. It was owned by a Russian oligarch, and his daughter both ran it and decorated it. The gimmick was beds: instead of tables, she placed large, luxurious beds around the interior, where patrons could lounge and order bottle service.

In terms of style, Duvet really was beautiful. They spent millions on it, even installing an enormous fish tank filled with exotic species and encrusted with real Swarovski crystals that spanned the entire length of the venue. But for whatever reason, it just didn't click. Partying there didn't feel special. All the gimmicks (and all the cash) couldn't keep patrons interested, and Duvet went to sleep forever, about a year after its opening.

Quo

Quo joined a row of nightclubs on 27th Street in Chelsea, a little bit late to the game, and lasted just over a year. The owner, Gary Malholtra, was an obscure finance/attorney guy, trying to make his dream of owning a nightclub into a reality. He sank millions into high-end decor, but really went all-out on a crazy-sophisticated sound system.

The sound system was technically amazing, but in terms of creating a great party, it didn't move the needle at all. No one cared about it, and with little more to offer, the place ended up an empty wasteland after the first six months. Of all the nightclubs that came and went, Quo was most notable as a prime example that no amount of money can buy that unmistakable feeling of coolness and excitement that people look for in a nightclub.

Pretty Is as Pretty Does

The nightclub industry folks played another important role in selling the feeling, and their strategies were as colorful and varied as the people themselves. I can recall a ton of promoters, club owners, and door people who were super successful, not because of their looks, but because of their personalities. They ranged from not-so-great-looking to beaten-with-the-ugly-stick, but even so, they had crowds of good-looking, smart, sophisticated people following them.

Why? Well, in many cases, these guys were just fun to be around! Ballsy, charismatic, approachable, social to a fault—they were successful because they knew how to connect with people on an instinctive level. In other cases, successful promoters might not be very fun or likable, but they sold people on qualities like competence, intelligence, or just sheer persistence. They worked, innovated, threw their weight around, flattered the right people, got in people's faces, and made nightlife their way of life. Determined to find success, they ultimately did.

Jean Claude the Funkypirate

One guy I remember in particular was the self-styled "Jean Claude the Funkypirate." He was a tall, skinny Black guy who always rocked an absurd and colorful outfit, topped off by a pirate hat (and if he were in the mood, an eye patch). Any given night, you could go out and find him living it up in the best clubs in NYC.

What did he do? I don't know. Who was he working for? No clue. How did he make money? A mystery. It didn't really occur to me to ask him—I was too busy either having fun or working myself! The main thing about Jean Claude the Funkypirate was that he brought the party, wherever he went.

That was the feeling he sold effortlessly. Anytime he showed up, the party suddenly got that much hotter, crazier, and more fun. People greeted him like a celebrity, jockeying for position to say hi and have a drink with him. He greeted them back (whether he knew them or not) and basked in his unquestioned status as a nightlife celebrity, beloved by owners, bouncers, doormen, and A-listers everywhere.

Johnny Premier

Johnny Premier, on the other hand, sold a different kind of feeling. This guy definitely proved that being a promoter was not a matter of Brad Pitt-like good looks: appearance-wise, he was kind of a skinnier Chris Farley. Nevertheless, he made a bundle of money over the years, solely because of his persistence.

Johnny ran a homemade, almost nonfunctioning website called The Premier List, which included a registration form aimed at getting users to subscribe to his "Johnny Premier Guestlist." It was basically a wannabe (and weird) copycat version of JoonBug, but while Ariana and I let our brand speak for itself, Johnny featured himself front and center on all his promotional materials.

JoonBug didn't really deal with Johnny much, but there was one night in the early days of JoonBug when we had a very memorable encounter with him. Ariana and I had just finished an event at a club called Discotheque, and we were standing around outside the owner Paul Drohan's door with a few others, including Johnny, waiting to get paid.

As usual, Johnny was wearing a white T-shirt that was much too small and unable to fully contain his belly, which protruded gently over the waistband of his black jeans.

After about half an hour of waiting, we were all feeling tired and a little agitated, when suddenly, Johnny did the totally unexpected and pulled a vial of coke out of his jacket pocket. Dramatically, he made a line on a table and ripped it up through his nose. We all stared at him in shock.

Turning to face us, he broke the silence. "You know who I am?" he bellowed. "That's right! I'm the heavyweight champion of all promoters!" With that, he raised his arms over his head in a gesture of triumph, and we saw that he was wearing a big, fake WWF championship belt around his waist. Until then, his stomach had completely hidden it from view.

Next, Johnny tore the belt off and held it aloft, circling around the room like Hulk Hogan after a victory in the ring, roaring that he was the champion. "No other promoters can beat Johnny Premier!" In a few choice words, he added that JoonBug, in particular, was nothing compared to the Premier List.

Ariana and I stood there with our mouths hanging open for a moment. Then we looked at each other, and somehow the utter insanity of it all hit us hard. We started laughing helplessly. The more we laughed, the more he yelled, until we were practically on the floor laughing with tears in our eyes while he stomped and shouted, and then began systematically and viciously kicking the door with all his strength.

The door opened. Paul stood there silently, a huge bouncer at his right hand. Neither of them said a word; the bouncer simply aimed one solid punch at Johnny's chest, and Johnny hit the floor like a ton of bricks. The rest of us froze.

Quietly, Paul wished Ariana and me a good evening and held out our pay envelope. We grabbed it and got out of there.

And Johnny? In spite of everything, his unstoppable persistence paid off. His sloppy appearance and penchant for drugs (and pro wrestling) didn't get in the way of his bulldoggish approach to promotions, which ultimately made him a success in the industry. He made it clear that he could always bring in a crowd, and club owners recognized and respected that—even if the type of crowd he brought in was scraping the bottom of the barrel. In fact, for club owners who were desperate to make the most of their dwindling popularity, that was a valuable service, and it became a specialty of Johnny's.

Jon B.

One of the genuinely coolest, as well as most successful, industry guys I know is Jon Bakhshi, more widely known as Jon B. He's a short, dark, stout, hairy-yet-balding Persian-Jewish guy with a loud mouth and a genius for making everyone love him. In terms of looks, he was average at best. In terms of charisma, he was unstoppable!

He was also incredibly smart. At NYU, he went to the Gallatin School, an elite program that was far superior to the College and Arts of Sciences that I attended. We often went out together, and at that time he was probably the most popular guy at NYU. This was no small feat, because the campus was and is enormous, and standing out there isn't easy.

Jon was always social in the extreme, super memorable, and fun to be around. He had a whole stock of one-liners that he threw out while meeting and greeting. Two of his favorites were, "Why don't you call me anymore?" and "Don't worry about it, you'll read about it in the papers tomorrow!" A consummate party animal, no one could resist his charm, and he would work himself into a literal sweat getting everyone at an event to dance the night away.

All of this served him well in his career as a nightlife professional. He didn't need movie-star looks or an ultra-suave demeanor to achieve incredible success. He needed intelligence, charm, and energy, and he had all three in spades. Over time, he became one of the biggest promoters in all of New York City. He was head of promotions at Cheetah, director of Show, and opened two venues on West Chelsea's 27th Street that were tremendously successful and long lived: Home and Guest House.

Craig Koenig

During high school, a couple of my friends were already getting started as promoters by running alcohol-free "Teen Parties" at nightclubs and other venues on the occasional Saturday night. These parties were as bad as they sound: banal, awkward, and vanilla. I occasionally went to a few, but it felt like I was basically at high school, at night, in a big event space. There was none of the diversity, maturity, coolness, or magic I had grown addicted to in the real NYC nightlife scene.

There was, however, an insane amount of money to be made, and Craig Koenig had it down to an art.

Tall, pale, and slightly bug-eyed, Craig was an average-looking Ashkenazi kid from Great Neck with a halo of curly brown hair that he usually hid under a Yankees cap. Jeans and a T-shirt, sometimes adorned with a team logo and sometimes not, were his daily uniform. Even as a teenager, he was a heavy smoker, going through packs and packs of Camels every week, and whenever we hung out, he always had a vodka soda nearby that he'd occasionally take a sip from. Total disregard for style (and a constant perfume of cigarette smoke and alcohol) might not seem like a recipe for being popular, but in Craig's case, none of that mattered at all.

The thing about Craig was that he was honestly just a super nice guy. He had a quality of harmlessness and trustworthiness that was disarming and relaxing to be around. Girls loved him, and he always had a hot blonde girlfriend who'd be super into him.

He was also smart, far beyond his years. He had an insanely profitable system in place for packing out his events, the main strategy being that he would recruit three or four of the most popular high school guys and girls to be his "party hosts." He made invites with their names at the top to create some prestige and offered to pay these "hosts" five bucks a head for every kid who came to the party using their invites.

Between a thousand and two thousand kids would usually show up. There were no alcohol costs; the kids usually paid the bar or club for soft drinks. With admission prices at around $25, and the costs for the event space and DJ costing only a few thousand dollars, I estimate that Craig was making somewhere in the neighborhood of $30,000 per party. In cash.

Even today, that would be a crazy amount of dough for a high schooler to make, and back then it was unbelievable. The "Party Hosts" didn't know any better and were happy with the few hundred dollars he'd throw at them for helping promote the party.

He used the same technique during prom season, which lasted a few months in the city. Each high school would typically have their prom on a different night of the week, so he would throw a ton of parties and make a ton of money during those times.

In college, he became the head of promotions for several clubs, including Chaos, a bar and lounge in Soho that was very popular and hard to get into.

After Chaos closed down, Craig moved on to Opera, a new club in West Chelsea. It was half dance floor and half lounge, and also, as I've mentioned, where Ariana and I met. After that, he opened his own nightclub, which he called 17. It was on 17th Street in Chelsea and became a very popular spot for J.A.P.s (Jewish American Princesses) from Long Island and New Jersey.

Ultimately, Craig was super successful because of his incredible business acumen, bolstered by his genuine likeability and easygoing personality. He might not have created a celebrity-like persona, but he built up a literal fortune in the world of nightlife!

Noah Tepperberg

One of the most famous and successful of all the promoters from that time was Noah Tepperberg. Now, he's lauded as a nightlife and hospitality guru to such an extent that he even teaches a course on it at Harvard. He and his business partner, Jason Strauss, are the heads of TAO Group Hospitality, which owns arguably the largest, most successful set of nightlife and hospitality venues in the country and abroad. Their venues include Marquee (in New York, Las Vegas, Singapore, Sydney, and other big cities globally), TAO Nightclub Las Vegas, Lavo (NYC, Las Vegas, and elsewhere), Avenue (Los Angeles and NYC), and a host of others.

But before they were the ultimate kings of nightlife, these guys were just two ordinary, preppy, studious Jewish teenagers, mostly notable for their intelligence.

Like Jon B., Noah was a guy who was balding a little bit even in high school (these days, he's rolling with the shaved-head look). Short, chubby, and pale, he was always businesslike and not exactly what you'd call a sparkling personality. However, by teaming up with the right people, building a stellar reputation, and putting his business acumen to use, he built a nightlife empire.

Over the course of his career, Noah developed a great reputation for being fair, taking his work seriously, paying well, and of course, having a clear and ambitious vision and bringing that vision to life. As you can imagine, all of that was much more important than his personal appearance, or even his personality.

In an industry where even the most profitable ventures are typically short-lived, Noah built lasting partnerships and created brands that have endured. The second nightclub Noah and his partners opened, Marquee in NYC, is probably the longest-running nightclub in the history of the city. It opened over eighteen years ago and is *still* considered a hotspot. Insane!

Faces, Feelings, and JoonBug

When it came to the "looks" side of working in nightlife, JoonBug took a very specific approach. In terms of interacting with club patrons and subscribers, we didn't have a "look," and never showed our faces as part of the brand. Industry people knew us, of course, but we didn't bother with putting our photos on the website or in the "About" section. Why? Because looks don't matter. Our subscribers weren't opening the JoonBug newsletter to see what Ariana and I looked like.

We wanted to build up the JoonBug brand as its *own* entity, separate from our personal names and fame. I was already thinking that one day, we would want to sell the business, and it wouldn't be worth much if the whole thing depended on me or Ariana being there.

But when it came to dealing with industry professionals, Ariana and I purposely cultivated a professional image. JoonBug was a business, and we took that seriously, always making sure to look put together and to be well-spoken. We came to meetings with a portfolio book, hard data charts, and photos to demonstrate our prior successes. Owners weren't used to that, and it made them consider our proposals (and high prices!) more seriously.

Another looks-related asset that we had was being a guy-girl team, and we learned to use that to our advantage, as well. It seemed like owners and promoters would always take more to one of us. I seemed to click best with guys like Noah Tepperberg, who were mostly interested in getting down to business. (Also, I later found out that Chris

Malm from Guastavino's had apparently chosen to work with JoonBug over some other promoters because he thought I was cute and liked the way I dressed. Good thing I wore that suit to the first meeting! Had I not, it literally could have changed the course of my life!)

Other people, of course, preferred to work with Ariana. She mostly worked with other women in the industry, but oftentimes guys also preferred to work with her over me. There just weren't many women in the nightlife business besides dancers, cocktail girls, coat-check girls, and bartenders. So, when an opportunity to meet with a well-dressed and pretty young woman came up, many owners would naturally rather take that opportunity than have me show up holding the portfolio book!

Meeting Seth

I remember in our second year of JoonBug, we were trying to secure the venue Capitale, which had just opened in the Bowery and was extremely popular. It was a former bank, absolutely stunning inside and able to hold thousands of patrons. I had tried several times to get a meeting with one of the owners, Seth Greenberg, but he wouldn't even take my call.

Ariana and I decided that the best approach would be to show up in person when Capitale was open. We would just show up, and keep showing up, until Seth showed up. That Friday night, we put on our best outfits and headed over. It turned out that we had chosen the right night. He was already at the bar, speaking with some of his employees.

Seth was, arguably, a very good-looking guy, considerably older than us, but with a great style. He was soft-spoken, carried himself well, and generally seemed like a person you'd want to be friends with. As we approached him, somehow I just knew that he would take to Ariana more than me. I gave her a subtle push in front of me and murmured, "Trust me. You lead and start talking to him." Without missing a beat, she put on an engaging smile and kept walking toward him. He stared at us cautiously at first, but when he saw Ariana smile, he smiled, too, and visibly let his guard down.

I didn't say a word during that whole meeting. Ariana did all the talking, and I just chilled off to the side. Occasionally, Seth would glance toward me, but I just sort of pretended not to be involved, and it seemed to work; he talked to Ariana for almost an hour, not about anything to do with JoonBug, but about him, and all his new projects, and how great Capitale was, and anything else that would stroke his ego (without getting sexual, of course!).

By the end of their conversation, Ariana had set up a meeting with him for the following morning to take over Capitale for Halloween and New Year's Eve, the two biggest nights for clubs.

The next meeting went very similarly; Ariana took the lead, sitting close to Seth and showing him our press book and photos of events that we had done, while I stayed in my seat practically separate from the two of them. I let her do all the talking, knowing that my job was to sit tight and let her work her magic. Let me tell you, Seth couldn't keep his eyes off her. As she leafed through the book to show him all the great stuff we had done, he didn't even glance at the pages! He just kept nodding and smiling, and when Ariana got done, he called in the GM.

"This is Ariana from JoonBug," he said. "She will be handling Capitale's Halloween and New Year's parties, and I'd like you to work on whatever she will need to make it a success."

Thanks to Ariana and our guy/girl team approach (and, in

part, to my knowing when to check my ego at the door and shut up), we were making big strides, and we were doing it all with hardly anyone even knowing who we were or what we looked like. For all they knew, there was simply a red bug with black spots taking over the nightlife industry, one bit (and one byte) at a time. It was challenging to put together the events at Capitale, but they were hugely successful. We sold over 5,000 tickets for each, made more money than ever, and felt like we were on top of the world. To top it all off, our press kit was now even more impressive, and so we were able to use it to get even more venues and expand the business.

Everybody's Doing It

Of course, owners and promoters weren't going to work with us solely because we looked professional or seemed well-spoken. Much more importantly, JoonBug itself had to seem successful, proven, and well-accepted in the industry. This was much easier as time went on and we gathered clippings and portfolio pieces. But in the beginning, we had to find more creative ways of selling that feeling. So, we deliberately tapped into two things: data and human nature. It was digital manipulation meets psychological warfare!

As far as human nature went, I knew that we had to appeal to people's sense of vanity and FOMO (fear of missing out). So, to create the illusion that JoonBug was well-established in the scene, we started out by promoting events for free, and in some cases without even asking. We sent our photographers to the hottest clubs in the city, listed their parties on our site and in our email blasts. All of this gratis, without asking permission and without letting them know. Next, we made sure to send those email blasts to all the club owners and promoters, as well as to our subscribers.

In no time, all the industry people were getting a serious case of FOMO! They'd see an email with amazing promotions for a major hotspot and get nervous that they weren't running the same type of promotions themselves. I could practically feel them thinking, if Noah and Jason are doing it, we should be doing it too!

It's one of the simplest yet most powerful tricks in the book. Having all of the hottest clubs in our roster legitimized us in our clients' eyes and led to big business. No one realized that those first ads weren't paid for! And in a different way, the promotions helped build trust with our client base. Through JoonBug, they could not only find out the best places to go out but could also catch glimpses into the most exclusive venues, establishing us as a legitimate authority in nightlife.

A Picture Is Worth 1,000 Words (And Then Some)

It's hard to emphasize how crucial photos were to our business. Our website, email newsletter, and special email blasts all included photos from the events we featured, and we made sure to use the best ones we could get (or make).

For recurring weekly events, we would showcase the best pictures from the previous week. Big holiday events like Halloween and New Year's Eve parties had the best photos from the previous year. It was important to have photos of beautiful people, and of course, beautiful women in particular. That's what sold the party! If everyone thought the event was going to be full of handsome men, gorgeous women, models, and celebrities, it would inevitably do well.

However, sometimes the previous events didn't have celebrities or great photos. Maybe not a lot of people had shown up, or the ones who did show weren't particularly striking. In that case, we had a simple (if sneaky) workaround: we just used photos from *other* events. Nobody could tell the difference, as long as the photo didn't have any identifying evidence in the background. Patrons just want to see a spectacular crowd having a blast, and that's what we showed them.

In the very early days of JoonBug, Ariana and I didn't have many photos to do this with, so we had to make our own. In a real pinch, I even swiped and used random photos from the internet! But more often, we would create our own "crowd" by inviting as many of our friends as we could to a given event, comping them with drinks and food. Then we'd have a bunch of pictures taken with them, and voilà! Perfect fodder for the JoonBug site. Ariana had lots of friends from the Fashion Institute of Technology who looked great in real life, and even better in pictures, so the site looked super appealing. None of our users knew that the people at the party were just our friends—and I don't think our friends knew any better, either!

Later in the JoonBug lifecycle, we used not only pictures, but video as well. For larger events like New Year's Eve, we would take hours of raw footage and have our editors professionally edit it all down to just a few minutes.

It was a big game changer. Video magnified our users' FOMO exponentially, while appealing to their sense of vanity and wanting to be cool. With video, we sold out huge venues in just a week or two, as opposed to a period of several months. That made it hands-down one of the most compelling and effective marketing tactics we ever used.

Party On

One of the required fields on our sign-up form was the user's birthday. Everyone gave it to us, and part of the reason we needed it was for age verification; users had to be at least eighteen to use the site.

Of course, people might lie about their birth year. But very few would lie about their birth month, and that turned out to be huge for JoonBug, because one of the most effective tactics we developed was sending "Happy Birthday" emails customized and personalized to each of our subscribers.

About two weeks before their birthday, we would send our subscribers an email with the subject line, "Happy Birthday {First Name}, let us help you celebrate for free and in style!" The sender was usually Liz@JoonBug.com, or Brooke@JoonBug.com. Liz and Brooke were Ariana's and my assistants, and the emails included their numbers and other details. That way, even though it was all automated, the subscribers felt like Brooke or Liz had sent personal, individualized emails. That strategy has been widely mimicked and is now standard practice in email marketing, but back then, it was novel. Users genuinely thought they were receiving a unique personal email from Brooke or Liz and almost always opened them!

The return rate was fantastic. Over 75 percent replied via email or phone, wanting to take advantage of our offer and set up a birthday party out on the town.

All those birthday celebrations were very lucrative for us, as well as for the clubs. Clubs loved birthday parties, because the birthday guy or girl basically acted like a club promoter, inviting dozens of their friends to come celebrate. And those friends, because the invite was personal and coming from someone they know, would usually show up with their proverbial party hats on, ready to party until dawn (and spend money freely). So, we worked out arrangements with various venues in which they paid us a monthly referral fee, and in exchange, we recommended them to our clients who wanted to set up parties.

We capped our number of referral clubs at about ten, so that we could hit a guaranteed and significant quota of leads on their behalf. With each club's fee at about two grand, we were making an easy $20,000 per month on referrals alone.

And for the partiers? They also won big: the birthday guys and girls got referrals to great venues, where they and a guest would be comped and given a free drink. It was a great deal for everyone involved, but especially for JoonBug!

Social Proof

JoonBug's success was definitely a case of selling feelings first and foremost. Sure, we had a killer approach to promotions, but we were also a startup doing radically new (and therefore untested) things in the industry. That in itself was bound to stir up skepticism and even resistance.

So, we intentionally set about creating an impression of authenticity. We stirred up people's FOMO and crafted sleek, enticing, visually driven marketing materials using whatever means necessary. On top of that, we provided our subscribers with super-valuable information, made our clients happy by filling their events with custom-tailored crowds, and paved the way for nightlife enthusiasts to have a great time, night after night.

We sold everyone on the feeling of our unquestionable authority, proven ability, and just a hint of exclusivity. As a result, JoonBug's success was taking off like a rocket! We felt unstoppable, and the more success we experienced, the more excited we were to chase that momentum and push things further.

That momentum is because of social proof. Most people are followers, not leaders. They want to be given cues that make deciding on a course of action clear and easy. In the case of event promotions, you have to give patrons the impression that the event you're throwing is somewhere they want to be. You have to tell them that it's going to be a great party, *without* telling them that it's going to be a great party!

If you can sell that perception effectively, as JoonBug did with our photos and other strategies, then not only will patrons show up—they'll inadvertently become promoters themselves, telling their friends, "I'm going to this great party, and you should come too!" And when that line of eager partiers forms at the door, anyone who sees it will want to get in as well. At that point, the hype is a self-fulfilling prophecy: everyone is so sure this will be a great party, that they create an amazing night with their energy and enthusiasm.

Of course, you have to take care of the basics: food, drinks, music, crowd size. But a beautiful venue and great decorations are far less important than the party-goers' starry-eyed perception of the event and each other. It doesn't matter what the venue looks like inside, or where it's located. It's all about selling that feeling.

Nightlife Lessons Learned

In nightlife, the only thing that matters is the feeling you have when you walk into the venue. Do you love the music? Do you love the ambience? Are you treated like a VIP? Is it a place you'd want to put on your social media?

The same goes for most businesses. It doesn't matter how big you are, what you look like, how many people work for you, or how much money you spent on your office space. What matters is your work ethic, the company you keep, the logistics and systems that make it work, and ultimately the results you get.

When EZ Texting was just getting started, I rented a small office in the Kaufman Building at 34th Street and 7th Avenue. I would walk into work in a hoodie, T-shirt, ripped jeans, and sneakers—a prototypical tech look that, at that time in New York, wasn't normal. Plus, I was often ruffled from working long hours. The lawyers and professionals in $10,000 suits and wearing fancy watches would see me and know that I was working in a really small, bare-bones office rather than one of their executive suites with glass doors and receptionists. They were looking down on and dismissing me. But we were already making a lot of money and were about to make a lot more.

The reason for our success? Nothing to do with looks. It was all about creating the feeling our customers wanted and needed. We stayed true to our name and did everything possible to make the system extremely easy to use. Complicated software makes you feel like crap, so we focused on providing the core functionality that people wanted in a very simple, easy-to-understand way. If you can make software an enjoyable and accessible experience, people will look forward to using it.

To that end, EZ Texting gamified all the technical things that are usually hard for most people to understand. During demos, one of the first things we would do is have the prospective customer send themselves an SMS. Their phone would buzz—and the proverbial lightbulb would go off above their head! They'd have a visceral, direct experience of exactly what our product did. Remember, this was 2006 and 2007, and things like texting access authentication codes, or even texting peer-to-peer, weren't nearly as common then.

Now, as a venture capitalist, I am focused both on the feeling I give to the founders of companies I'm thinking of funding and the feeling I get from them. It's not a judgment based on how they look or other superficialities. In fact, some of the smartest business guys aren't necessarily all that eloquent, nor do they have the best pitch decks. Digging past internal biases can help you find some real gems in the rough.

The fact is that venture capitalism is, in large part, a guessing game. Anyone who tells you that they can predict the next big business is full of it. As a VC, you're really betting on the team, the idea, the total addressable market and the product market fit. And even after doing all the necessary research, it's ultimately the feeling you get and give that tips the scale.

LESSON 4

YOU'RE ONLY AS GOOD AS YOUR LAST PARTY

IN THE WORLD OF NIGHTLIFE, no one cares what you did before. They only care about what you're doing now. You might have made magic last year, but if this year has been a bust, that's what people will remember—especially in today's short-term-memory, social-media-focused, "everyone gets a trophy" world!

That's why you always have to be on your A-game. Being consistent in representing yourself in a positive light and providing a quality product will fuel your stamina on the social circuit as well as in business. While it's great if you can start a thriving business and sell it for a ton of cash, remember: if you can't make it happen again, you'll quickly fade out.

Suite 16 Turns Sour

JoonBug's first year had several amazingly great parties, some mediocre ones, and a few that were complete flops. We learned how to cope financially by reducing our risks, and we learned to cope emotionally by focusing on the next event or revenue-generating feature, rather than constantly harping on the past (although it was still important to learn from our mistakes).

The events that were just duds, the ones that no one came to for whatever reason, were often the most difficult to deal with emotionally, far worse than well-attended events that turned into logistical disasters. Throwing a huge party that no one comes to creates a unique kind of despair, a dread that maybe your prior successes were just a lucky streak—one that's now over.

Thursday, Thursday

In the second year of JoonBug, we took on a weekly Thursday night party at Suite 16. Noah Tepperberg and Jason Strauss were running things. They were the club's face and owned a small percentage but were not the actual owners.

We were really looking forward to doing these parties, because Suite 16 was one of the hottest, most exclusive venues in the city. If we could do a great event there, it would help build our brand and legitimize our reputation, not only with our online following but also with club owners and promoters. We went all out trying to make the first night a big success. We sent out a big email blast to our entire NYC database, with a professionally designed digital flyer. A special second invite went out to about a thousand handpicked VIP recipients—not as a blast, but individually and personally, one email at a time.

We also hired a couple of people to distribute physical copies of our flyers outside Suite 16 on Friday and Saturday nights for several weeks, figuring that people who went there on the weekends would likely come on a weekday, too. Finally, we spent the few days leading up to the first party inviting people by phone.

Black Swan Sighted

The big night finally came around: March 20, 2003. It seemed like we had it in the bag—a superhot venue, no detail overlooked, every kind of promotion you could do, and on top of that, Thursdays in general were a big night to go out. (It would have been much harder to do parties on Mondays or Tuesdays, for example.)

Still, both Ariana and I were very nervous, so we decided to get some of our energy out and head to the club early. When we arrived, the staff were setting up and the DJ was doing sound checks, everything exactly on schedule. We walked around, checking out the venue, and decided to have a drink to calm our nerves.

At that moment, our door guy, Jimmy the off-duty cop, arrived. It was 9:30 p.m., and the doors were set to open at 10 p.m. Jimmy had been working for us for a while, doing the door for us at Guastavino's and Veruka on a regular basis. He was from Queens with a thick, New York accent, and he always looked well-groomed and put together in a suit or a leather jacket and jeans.

Coming up to us, he wore a very serious expression and cleared his throat uncomfortably. "Not sure if you heard the news, but we just invaded Iraq. I hope that doesn't affect us too much tonight."

I glanced at Ariana, and then told Jimmy I thought we would be fine. Maybe a few people would be scared, but after all, this was

New York City. People in New York have thrown parties despite much worse news—in fact, the worse the news, the more resilient and determined New Yorkers are to defy the odds and have fun.

That's what I told Jimmy, but looking back, I think I was telling it more to myself. I was worried, and rightfully so.

Missing Persons

Over the next few hours, nothing eventful happened. We set up the ropes outside, but the line had not yet started to form. We waited.

Minutes ticked by, but still no one came into the venue. I kept going back out to see what was going on, since the place felt eerily empty. The DJ was playing great music to a crowd that consisted of a few bartenders, our servers, and a coat check girl. I thought maybe things were just a little slow. After all, sometimes people just didn't show up until the doors had been open for a bit.

But by eleven o'clock, I was pacing around, feeling super rattled. The photographer had taken about five photos of me and Ariana and a few other people working that night, and after that, with nothing else to do, had seated himself at a banquet and started reading a book with the aid of a small flashlight. Ariana and Jimmy both said we should cut our losses and go home. It was a complete and utter failure, and I think it was the first time ever that not one single person had shown up to one of our parties, or to one of Suite 16's events.

The manager, looking around at the empty room in disbelief, demanded to know what was going on, and where the heck all our people were. "Why did I bother opening the place and staffing it if you aren't going to bring people?" he sputtered. We were at a loss for words. I tried to formulate some kind of excuse, telling him how hard we had worked, and how this had never happened to us before, yada yada yada. But in the end, I just told him straight up that we were sorry and weren't sure what had happened, or why. I told him I would talk about it with Noah and Jason the next day. We left at midnight.

As we walked out, Jimmy could see the dejection on my face. "Hey, don't worry," he said reassuringly. "You guys will figure it out, and this is going to be a crazy Thursday-night party. It happens to the best of them."

Driving Force

His words didn't help. That night, I felt the smallest I had in a long time, and for days afterward, I doubted whether I should even be in the nightlife business, or if anyone would come to any of our parties again. We had been on such a winning streak with all the different parties and website features and digital ads that this sudden, abrupt failure totally humbled me.

It didn't matter if anyone else was judging me by this last party. *I* was judging me, and I was my harshest critic. That incident instilled a special kind of fear of failure in me and in Ariana. In the world of events especially, I knew that you could be hot one day but old news the next. It drove us to stay far away from complacency. From that day, we were determined to push forward, try new things, hedge our bets with multiple parties and revenue streams, and always get back up and try again harder—with any and every setback we would inevitably have.

Romantic Comedy (of Errors)

In 2004, the very next year, we had a nearly zero-guest dud for the second time. And we not only lost face, but also a lot of money, betting on a night that we were sure would be a big success: Valentine's Day.

Big Night, Big Money

Ariana and I were always on the lookout for "big nights" where lots of people would go out and party. Big crowds meant big money, so New Year's, Halloween, Thanksgiving Eve, St. Patrick's Day, Christmas Eve, and all the rest were our top event nights. It only seemed logical to add a big Valentine's Day bash to the roster, and in 2004, we went for it. We found the perfect venue for it, too—Duvet.

As I described before, Duvet was a venue bedazzled in Swarovski crystals, with gorgeous wrap-around fish tanks that showcased gleaming tropical fish and bioluminescent jellyfish. Instead of banquets and tables, rich and ritzy beds were strategically placed across the entire club. It definitely had a luxe and romantic vibe that we thought would be perfect for the occasion.

Sky's the Limit

We got to work, designing the ultimate Valentine's night out. We hired Sky Nellor as the DJ. At that time, she was charging around five grand per night, which was more than twice the typical fee. But she was one of the first female celebrity DJs of the time, a former model/actress whose name alone would draw a crowd. With Sky there, we were sure that people would be sure to swarm to the venue—if only in the hopes of seeing other models and actors there along with her!

We had a bunch of Valentine's-themed gimmicks lined up as well, like free champagne and chocolate-covered strawberries. Tickets cost $20 in advance, or $40 at the door, to incentivize people to purchase ahead. But strangely, by the day of the event, we had only sold about ten tickets online. That's right, ten.

We rationalized that maybe this was the kind of event where most people show up and pay at the door, but it was not to be. We were way too optimistic and stunningly wrong. Not even half of the ten people who bought tickets online actually showed, and no one else came *at all*. It was another night of great music, a great venue, great everything, but all for nothing. We were filled with embarrassment, depressed, and felt that we looked bad not only to the owner (who lost money staffing the place), but to Sky, who was super surprised to be playing to an empty room. The five people who did show up left about half an hour later in disappointment.

Unlucky in Love

In retrospect, it was a very cheesy and not a well-thought-out idea. People who have dates on Valentine's Day don't want to come out to a club—that really isn't very romantic, no matter what kind of gimmick you try to sell them on! Therefore, anyone who *did* come to our party was more or less admitting that they didn't have a date for Valentine's Day, which was super embarrassing and not fun.

Sadly, we didn't figure that out at the time, and the following year we gave it another shot, this time at PM. The results were slightly better, but not by much, even though the venue was much smaller and ought to have sold itself. That night, we realized we should never do another Valentine's Day event again!

Photo Finish

One way we did save face with our failures was by manipulating the digital evidence. That was where having a ton of photos from other events came in handy! We got creative, if a bit deceptive, and posted some carefully selected photos from other events at those venues, giving the appearance of success. We were mainly worried about what other promoters and venue owners would think and less worried about the public. Honestly, it would have been much easier to just delete the events from the website than to go through the trouble of curating misleading pictures. But we needed to give owners and promoters the impression that our parties were consistently fun and, more importantly, filled with paying customers.

The Botched Ball

Probably the most outrageous disaster of a party that I can recall happened in our first year. After JoonBug did our initial Halloween event at Guastavino's, other promoters started to notice the place. Our regular Saturday night parties and our help in setting up regular Friday night parties there added to the buzz. It wasn't long before my friend Craig Koenig approached me about setting up a meeting with Chris and Artan. He wanted to propose doing a Guastavino's New Year's Eve party.

I was happy to help him out and set up the meeting, which went so well that by the end of it, they had a handshake deal. Craig and his business partner at the time, a guy named Shlomi, would take over Guastavino's for New Year's Eve.

Tickets, Please

Ariana and I were so new to the game that we had no idea that New Year's Eve was a much easier and more lucrative event to sell tickets for than even Halloween. In any case, Craig and Shlomi tapped JoonBug to help sell tickets, so we were happy—at first.

Craig and Shlomi mostly sold their tickets through networks of sub-promoters, allocating a set of tickets to each one and paying them a cut of the revenue. If a sub-promoter couldn't sell all of his or her tickets, the unsold tickets were returned to Craig and Shlomi. If the sub-promoter sold out, he or she could usually get more tickets to sell.

The individual sub-promoters that Craig worked with were selling maybe twenty to fifty tickets each, but with our website, we quickly went through three hundred, and asked for more. Craig and Shlomi were kind of stunned and, instead of giving us more tickets, capped us at the three hundred we had sold—an unexpected and unwelcome turn of events for us! The other promoters were still trying to sell their tickets, and it was good business for Craig and Shlomi to keep them happy so that they could continue networking with them in the future. But the situation was frustrating all around. At JoonBug, we were getting calls and emails every day from people wanting to buy tickets, but we couldn't get our hands on any more to sell! I later realized that we should have been soliciting other promoters to sell tickets for their events and meet demand. That's what we did the next year, and it was extremely lucrative for us.

Despite being capped at way under our ability to sell, I did profit in other ways from working with Craig on that party. In particular, I learned some great tricks for negotiating favorable terms on a given event. Usually, by guaranteeing a certain revenue number, you can get whatever you really want in return. Later on, Ariana and I would take this idea even further and do whole buyouts of the venues we wanted, offering payment in advance. Paying for the venue in advance was unheard of back then and got us access to venues and terms way more favorable than we could otherwise have negotiated. It was a risky strategy, because if we weren't able to sell enough tickets, we would incur losses (sometimes heavy ones). But for the most part, we weighed the risks very carefully and got great returns on our investments.

Set 'Em Up, Knock 'Em Down

When New Year's Eve came around, we headed to Guastavino's a little early to check out how things were shaping up. Unfortunately, it quickly became obvious that Craig, Shlomi, and even Guastavino's itself were all completely unprepared for this type of event. It wasn't a simple party like Halloween, where all you need is a DJ, some lights, and drinks. This was a black-tie event with each ticket costing between $150 and $300. There were hors d'oeuvres, dinner stations, entertainment, a ball-drop showing on a big screen, coat check, champagne toast, and all the works! Not to mention bottle service tables with special dinner arrangements for people who had purchased the more expensive tickets.

Ariana and I walked through the doors at about seven that evening. The event was scheduled to start at eight, so there was just one short hour left to get everything ready … and it was complete mayhem. Not even half of what needed to be in place was ready (or there at all). The servers, bottle waitresses, and security were all disorganized, walking around aimlessly with no one to direct them. Coat check was set up in front of the entrance, with only one coat-check person to wait on the guests. The decorations weren't finished, the tables weren't set up—and there definitely weren't enough of them—and the hired entertainment wasn't even on site! Ariana, much more than I, knew what was in store. Speechless, she stared around wide-eyed, taking in the whole chaotic scene. Then she turned to me, and said simply, "This is going to be a disaster."

A Chilly Welcome

At eight o'clock, a line of patrons had formed and was already stretched around the block— it was probably double the size of the huge line we'd had at Halloween. To anyone in the know, it was painfully obvious that the event had been oversold. On top of that, the night was absolutely freezing, which meant that people would be even less patient than usual. No one wants to stand in line forever in their best black tie and high heels, let alone in the bitter cold of a New York City New Year's Eve.

Inside, Craig and Shlomi were running around like chickens with their heads cut off, and Ariana and I were hanging out uneasily by the bar, watching it all unfold. It wasn't our event, so we weren't going to grab the reins and start running things—and it would've been too late, anyway. The storm had begun, and there was no way to stop it. Craig and Shlomi had obviously put many more tickets out on the street than the venue could hold, assuming that most of the tickets would return to them unsold. But their tactic was about to backfire, majorly, because all those tickets had been snapped up! As soon as the doors opened, there was a huge traffic jam right at the entrance. With the coat check area stationed immediately in front of the doors, people who wanted to check their coats were forced to line up a second time as soon as they stepped foot in Guastavino's. The one coat-check person was frantically trying to wait on them all, and people started getting angry. It took some patrons over an hour and a half to get in, and by that time, they had to stop the line (which was still huge) because Guastavino's was at capacity. Security wouldn't let anyone else in, and people were literally standing right outside the double entrance and down the street, yelling, screaming, and freezing!

The Worst Game of Dominoes Ever

The yelling and screaming and freaking out continued inside, where things fell apart, one after another. Each fiasco seemed to spawn another, and then another, and then another. For the entire first hour, the DJ couldn't figure out how to work the sound system, so the music was basically a boring CD of some sort that sounded like elevator music. This, combined with the annoyance of the crowd, created a somber atmosphere with no energy.

By ten o'clock, the food stations were depleted. People who had expected hors d'oeuvres, or worse, dinner, were now having to be told that there wasn't anything to eat, which infuriated them. They complained loudly to anyone who would listen, including Chris,

Artan, Craig, and Shlomi. But there was nothing that could be done to fix the situation at that point. The only thing they could do was let people vent.

Meanwhile, the bar was a mob scene. Without enough staff, the crowd was three and four layers deep around a few flustered bartenders hurriedly pouring drinks and sloshing them toward the customers. After a while, some of them just threw up their hands, unable to cope with the nonstop pressure, demands, and complaints. You could see the look of defeat on their faces. It got so bad that I remember seeing Artan jump behind the bar and desperately start pouring drinks alongside them.

Before we knew it, the time was 12:05 a.m., but the DJ had forgotten to do the countdown. The big screen that was supposed to show the ball-drop was a blank rectangle, and there was no champagne toast. Disorganized, chaotic, and miserable, patrons inside and outside ranted and raved.

At 12:30, Ariana and I left, walking home past a huge line of people *still* waiting outside the venue. They had paid too much money to just walk away without at least getting in and getting some of their money's worth. I remember seeing one girl crying her eyes out, mascara dripping down her face, begging and pleading for security to let her in because her friends were all inside, and she hadn't brought a coat. On one of the coldest nights in NYC I can remember, she had been standing outside in a short, sleeveless dress and stiletto heels for over two hours.

As we passed by the head of security, a football-player-sized guy named Drew, he looked us straight in the eyes and said, "You guys are going to have a big mess on your hands tomorrow." We sighed and cringed. Although it wasn't our fault, we knew we'd have to deal with some of the aftermath of this debacle. The people who had bought tickets from us would inevitably complain. Sure enough, when we got home, there were already a few nasty and threatening emails waiting, and I could barely sleep after that.

Payback Time

Over the next few days, the news about Guastavino's New Year's Eve fiasco spread like wildfire. For JoonBug, it was a disaster that quickly grew frightening in its severity. Over a hundred people called and emailed JoonBug, demanding refunds. We did try to show goodwill and refund as many as we could afford. Despite our disclaimers and the fact that it wasn't our fault, we knew that the night had been a complete wreck for everyone. It was early days for JoonBug, and we didn't want to leave a bad taste in anyone's mouth. The issue was, we had already paid Craig and Shlomi, so we didn't have the money to refund everybody!

Then things took an even sharper downward turn. Because we had racked up so many complaints, PayPal suspended our account. This was a hard hit because PayPal was our only way of accepting credit cards at that time. On top of that, PayPal unilaterally elected to refund a bunch of people which made our account negative. They also issued a legal disclaimer that we had to pay the negative balance (over $10,000), or they would pursue us in court.

It was next to impossible to find the PayPal customer service phone number, but somehow I managed and tried to call and resolve things. Their representative was even more abrasive than the legal disclaimer they had sent! I spent hours on the phone, pleading and bargaining, but all I got for my efforts were legal threats and intimidation tactics. We had no recourse to respond to the complaints against us, and no way to prove that some of them were bogus.

In any case, their scare tactics worked. I was scared! We had never dealt with that much backlash and liability before. However, after thinking it over, I figured that they probably wouldn't actually sue us over that amount of money. Despite our anxiety, we left the PayPal account to deal with later and concentrated on finding other processors that would allow us to accept credit cards online.

Needless to say, we didn't make any money on that event. Ironically, the sub-promoters we had outsold ended up in the best position: most of them had sold their tickets for cash, and no one could call their credit card companies or leave bad reviews for them! Having a large business on the internet involves certain vulnerabilities, and those are two big ones.

Guastavino's was reeling too, as were Craig and Shlomi. Back then, CitySearch was the main local search engine that people used to find restaurants and other local businesses, and they had a review section that got flooded with over a thousand complaints about the party, bashing the venue and ripping Craig and Shlomi to pieces. I remember one in particular, because the title made me laugh out loud: "Blow me, Shlomi!" It got to the point that Guastavino's had to hire a lawyer to contest the negative reviews and get them removed from the site (I think the presence of the lawyer was all it took), and both Craig and Shlomi had to change their phone numbers. Although Craig would eventually recover and open his own nightclub, Shlomi never came back from that event.

Damage, Controlled

Ariana and I were sure that all the fallout had basically killed JoonBug. We thought that no one would ever set foot in Guastavino's again, especially for our Saturday night party. In fact, probably no one would *ever* come to *any* of our parties.

But we had to give it our best shot and pull out all the stops to salvage the business we had built. The week after New Year's, we called all our VIPs and friends personally and sent out two email blasts instead of one.

Some of our subscribers responded by immediately unsubscribing, and some sent nasty replies, telling us that our reputation was ruined in NYC. But when Saturday night came around, it seemed that somehow, miraculously, that party had survived unscathed!

It turned out that our Saturday night crowd, by and large, was not interested in upscale black-tie New Year's Eve events, and they weren't going on CitySearch to read reviews about Guastavino's, either. Most of them were regulars who had been coming for weeks or months, and they already knew that they could expect to have fun, hear great music, and party with a diverse crowd in a beautiful venue. They continued happily partying with us on Saturday nights, oblivious to the fiasco that had taken place just days prior.

Be Our Guest

The real test for us came the following year, around November. Artan and Chris approached us, hoping that JoonBug would be willing to take on New Year's Eve at Guastavino's that year. Our initial, knee-jerk reaction was a flat-out no. After the previous year's catastrophe, Guastavino's (on New Year's Eve, at least) was cursed! No promoter wanted to touch the place with a ten-foot pole.

But Artan and Chris were persistent, and after a second meeting, I was warming up to the idea that just maybe we could pull it off. Artan told us that he and Chris had learned from their mistakes, and that JoonBug would have complete control over the venue, waitstaff, security, and tickets. Plus, we wouldn't have to meet any minimums or lay out any money at all.

That made the deal almost irresistible for me, because even if we failed miserably, at least we wouldn't be hurt financially. But Ariana was still a "no." She really thought there was no way we'd sell even one ticket. I could see her perspective, but there were a few reasons I was starting to think it could work.

For one thing, we could promote it to our regular Saturday-night crowd since New Year's Eve was on a Saturday that year. Also, our database had grown tenfold since January—and all those new subscribers had no idea what happened the previous year. Plus, the legal team Guastavino's hired had been successful in getting most of the negative reviews taken down, so the online evidence was minimal.

Try, Try Again

Eventually, Ariana agreed, and we told Chris and Artan we'd give it a try. This time, we weren't taking any chances and put all our digital and event-planning know-how into making the night a huge success. Naturally, every promoter and venue owner in the city thought we were crazy, especially Craig and Shlomi. They all predicted failure, and some, the complete demise of JoonBug itself.

But we focused on our plans and tuned out the naysayers, making flyers, sending emails, and using one of our new strategies: calling hotel concierges. No one else was doing that, but for us, it was a great way to bring in people. Hotel guests were always asking concierges for nightlife recommendations, especially on New Year's, but the concierges didn't always have great answers, so working with them was a win for everyone.

As the party drew closer, we found (somewhat to our amazement) that ticket sales were going well. We were careful to sell under capacity, to avoid the fiasco of the year before, and ended up selling out with no problem! Many of our Saturday-night regulars bought tickets, as we had hoped. And, somewhat counterintuitively, we also sold tickets to a lot of people who had tried to get tickets the year before but failed because it had sold out so quickly. It seemed that they hadn't heard about how that party turned out. In any case, they were luckier this time around—in more ways than one!

New Year, New Party

Ariana spent three whole days prior to the event setting everything up, making sure everyone was properly prepared, and organizing all of the details. And just like with most of our other parties, everything went off without a hitch. Everyone had a great time, and New Year's Eve at Guastavino's made a hugely successful comeback. Not only that, JoonBug actually made the most money that night of any single event we had done to date. We had kept our ticket prices high, and our costs to Guastavino's were practically nil. We had defied the odds and rehabbed the reputation damaged by last year's bomb of a party with this year's hit of a party.

Nightlife Lessons Learned

If your last party was a failure, then you have a lot of work ahead of you! You can still turn things around by making your next party good—or even the best ever, why not? Will it be hard? Probably. Will it be risky? Definitely. But if you wait long enough for people to forget and take precautions to guarantee a good product, you can always have another shot at success.

And if your last party was a winner? Well, you still have a lot of work to do, because continuing to create, innovate, and bring quality products to market is always hard work. But the momentum of success is real and brings with it not only satisfaction, but also amazing opportunities you would never have found otherwise.

The same is true when it comes to building businesses and making investments. As a VC, I get judged by the last company I invested in and whether it was a big winner, mediocre investment, or a total bust. Yet there can be times when you have many bad investments in a row and for long stretches. That's how the chips fall sometimes because it's a probability game. But over time things should even out, and you have to have the temperament and emotional fortitude to keep on track and believing and making investments despite the fact that you doubt yourself and feel dejected. You might have nineteen bad investments in a row sometimes, but your twentieth one can hit big and more than make up for the nineteen previous bad ones.

Most people measure success by two different things—first, money (growing profits and revenue), and second, fame. When it comes to startups, the entrepreneurs that go for fame over money are the ones that go out of business first.

How others perceive your success is all about the optics and what you show to the world, as I discussed in lesson 1 on "How To be

Fake." But how you perceive your own success is more complicated—and can have more impact on your actual success.

You can be arguably very successful relative to everyone else but still feel rotten inside and unfulfilled. That can stem from many things but usually the root of it is fear. Fear of losing what you have, fear that you are an imposter, fear of success, fear of failure, and so on. That's what a lot of entrepreneurs have to struggle with and many never even come close to resolving. I think it's always a work in progress, but the ones that are the happiest know when they need to work on themselves.

It's hard not to psych yourself out, especially when you have multiple losses. Instead, you have to realize that it's all part of the game. Despite having numerous failed parties, I had to push myself to continue to try again.

I also think if you ruminate too much on your failures, you will fall down the rabbit hole of self-doubt. This constant self-doubt was one of my biggest struggles at JoonBug and later at EZ Texting, and I know many other entrepreneurs go through it. On one hand, it's the fear of losing that is often the driving force that keeps you in the game. But oftentimes it takes you down the rabbit hole and becomes mentally unhealthy, so you feel constantly unhappy and unfulfilled. The key is to learn to strike the balance to keep the fire going but not burn yourself and everyone around you out. And to surround yourself with people who will help you get out of your own head. With JoonBug, I luckily had Ariana to help me do just that.

A lot of times, you have to say to yourself, "This sucks, but I learned what I could from it and now it's time to try again." You can't outsmart negative emotions that come with inevitable failure. What's most important is being emotionally able to deal with the bad feelings that may last for long periods of time. Resilience is essential, but it's more than that. You can be resilient and still be depressed. What's the point of resilience if you're not happy?

That only comes with experience and knowing you've been through worse. I struggled a lot throughout my time at JoonBug with taking things too personally and always being on edge. So much so that I wasn't happy unless everything was perfect, and I was losing sleep over everything that went wrong. Much later in life, I came across stoicism, which has really influenced my attitude about all this. How important is this going to be after I'm dead? I ask myself that a lot.

A lot of people think of stoicism as apathy, but it's quite the opposite. Instead, its aim is to avoid the extremes and remind yourself that everything is temporary. Through a lot of practice, I've changed my self-talk during tough times to: Know it's temporary, remain equanimous, and then get back to work.

LESSON 5

IF YOU CAN'T BUY IT, BUILD IT

WHILE RUNNING JOONBUG, ESPECIALLY IN the beginning, there were a lot of business processes I knew could benefit from a digital upgrade. Many tasks could be done better, cheaper, or easier with the right software. Aside from upgrading existing systems, I also had other ideas for entirely new approaches that could only be implemented digitally.

Nowadays, finding software for nearly any kind of business process is relatively easy. In fact, sometimes the hardest part is choosing one tool out of numerous strong competitors. Almost anything you can imagine, you can get, thanks to a whole world of SaaS providers and API technology.

But in the 1990s and early 2000s, that ecosystem was in its infancy. There were many instances in which I faced a choice: continue doing business the old-fashioned, inefficient, analog way or build the tools I needed from scratch.

DIY Success

Because of my long-standing interest in computer science, coding, and software development, I was always on the lookout for ways that technology could improve the way we did business. I was obsessed with getting things done better than anyone else, whether that meant more efficiently, more professionally, more cheaply, more "whatever" the case might be. This turned out to be possibly the most important factor in JoonBug's success, and that's why I think that all founders today need to have a fundamental understanding of technology.

Being in the know about technology allows you to read between the lines and truly understand how to apply technology with maximum effectiveness. You might wonder if that really matters these days, when almost anyone can throw together a quick website using SquareSpace or use a decent SaaS to streamline their bookkeeping.

But the way I see it, you can compare this situation to doing robotic-assisted surgery. The robot is extremely "smart" and programmed to do the job expertly. It might seem that a relatively intelligent person with a basic knowledge of anatomy might be able to perform a successful surgery, while letting the robot control the process. But that's not really a good idea. You still need to have a fully trained surgeon who understands the process in depth.

Similarly, a founder can't effectively oversee the creation of a digital business without having a fundamental knowledge of programming: how computer chips, memory, browsers, and the internet work. The fact is, with the ubiquity of websites, social media, email and text marketing, and more, *all* businesses these days are essentially tech-oriented. Starting a business without at least basic tech knowledge is like starting a plumbing outfit with no knowledge of plumbing—you're sure to fail!

Some of the tech we had to build for JoonBug included our website and database, a homegrown CRM system for managing our A-list clients, and a state-of-the-art digital ticketing system that I enhanced to track inventory, integrate with shipping systems (like FedEx), generate labels, and make ticket fulfillment much easier.

But all of that was just the tip of the iceberg. There were countless business processes that we automated. Sometimes that meant customizing existing tech, and sometimes it meant building entire systems (most of which the public never saw) from the ground up. Here are a few of our technological assets and innovations, and the stories behind them.

Use It or Lose It

Let's start with the most basic ways we optimized our business. These mainly included existing tech that we utilized strategically for maximum benefit. After all, as great as it is to build your own technology, many times the best way to get ahead is to use what's already out there. Don't bother re-inventing the wheel—just customize the heck out of it!

The JoonBlog

When blogging became the *en vogue* thing to do around 2003, we jumped on the bandwagon right away. I thought about building a blogging system for JoonBug myself, especially since I had built what was basically one of the first blogging systems in the world during my time as lead developer at Convey.com. But luckily, before I got started building it out, I found TypePad, which had just launched that year. It had all the features we could ever want: custom domain, customizable colors, headers, and footers, and more. It wasn't clear to me exactly how we would monetize the blog, but I knew that "content is king" and we needed one. So, we started blogging and dubbed our new venture "The JoonBlog."

At first, we posted editorial-type pieces about events along with some curated photos. It was almost like running our own nightlife magazine. But it quickly became clear that the project was taking up too much time and too many resources. We didn't want to start a whole publishing business! To support the blog as it stood at that point, we would have had to start looking for editors, writers, and a slew of other staff.

However, we already had a great digital ad sales team in place, who were hard at work selling banners, emails, and custom placements, both online and offline. I thought about it and realized that if the blog could simply drive more traffic to our website, then we could make more of those sales. In other words, the blog would provide what is now called "content marketing."

So, we pivoted. With our new, refined goal of driving traffic in mind, we stopped writing editorial pieces and started writing tons of reviews. Basically, we reviewed all the bars, venues, nightclubs, lounges, and restaurants we worked with across New York, and in other hot cities like Miami and LA. Those pieces were way easier to write than full-blown articles and much more time efficient! We already had most of the contact info we needed, and the owners were more than happy to take photos for us and email them in. After all, it was free advertising for them!

From there, all we had to do was write up a generic review, using whatever info and photos we had, plus a little imagination. We never wrote a poor review, and we churned out dozens a day. Within a month, our blog entries were ranking No. 1 on Google for each of the venues we wrote about. Thanks to a combination of our website's high rank (JoonBug was already generating a ton of hits prior to the JoonBlog), each post's blog structure, and some other SEO tactics we had gotten super good at, we were outranking big names such as Zagat and CitySearch.

Within a few more months, we had posted literally thousands of reviews. Our website traffic had more than doubled, thanks to all the long-tail searches we were capturing for terms such as Marquee, Pacha, Cain, Bungalow 8, TAO, and other hot (or not-so-hot) search entries.

You've Got Mail!

With more traffic came more revenue—lots of it. There were two main mechanisms that we profited from: first, ad inventory on our website, and second, advertisements sent out to our email list.

As I've mentioned, we sold ads on the website itself, which was a huge moneymaker. As JoonBug grew, we had all kinds of advertisers, from major clubs to major brands such as Johnnie Walker, Mercedes, Tanqueray, American Express, Jaguar, and many others. These luxury and lifestyle brands were all eager to target the young and affluent demographic we specialized in serving.

Meanwhile, individual patrons and users who visited our site were usually funneled into some sort of signup flow that would allow us to collect their data. From there, we could monetize *them* by sending emails with ads. We had basically two email products: our "Weekly Buzz," which went out on Wednesdays and listed all the events coming up that week in a user's particular city, and our dedicated email blasts, which were entirely focused on one event or product.

Our clients and sponsors could purchase space in the Weekly Buzz or buy a dedicated blast. We had different price points, depending on where they wanted to place their ads in the Weekly Buzz. There were also a few different options for email blasts: segmenting the ad to various demographics or going with a "half blast" (sent to half our database) or "full blast" (sent to the entire list).

For email blasts, we came up with a clever price structure that was different for our two main groups: brands and clubs/owners/promoters. The market rate CPM (cost per thousand—mille—impressions) and size of our database was such that brands and sponsors such as Mercedes or American Express could expect to pay $50,000 or more for an email blast.

But there was no way a club or promoter could budget that much. And after all, our users were only reading our emails so that they could find out what was going on at a club, or to learn more about a particular event—not to see ads from American Express! So, there was a disconnect: although clubs and promoters couldn't pay the market rate like big brands could, they were the ones that had the content we actually needed.

With that in mind, we made the decision to drastically slash our prices for clubs, owners, and promoters, charging them about a tenth of the market rate. Everyone got their email blasts, users got the content they wanted, and JoonBug continued to bring in the profits and the data. It was a great deal for everyone!

Marketing Mavericks

Our SEO game was strong, earning us top ranking for keywords from "nightlife," "lounges," and "bars" to "Halloween party," "New Year's Eve Party," and "Thanksgiving Eve Party."

But we had another edge. We were super savvy when it came to Google AdWords. When we started running ads with AdWords, practically nobody else in the industry was even considering it. I think it was partly because the AdWords interface and system were complicated, and partly because many of the promoters and venue owners didn't yet have actual websites in place for users to click through to. So, they had no way of seeing how the ads performed. And finally, most of those guys were short-sighted, cheap, and didn't believe in paying for ads, especially if they didn't have a way to track their results.

Since we had practically no competition, many of the search terms we were bidding on cost next to nothing. It's totally different now—everyone and their mother is running ads, and the cost per click is through the roof! But back then, we were paying at most four cents per click, and the search volume for many of the terms was very high. We then took things a step further. We figured out how to arbitrage paying for clicks on Google at rock-bottom prices, while capturing much more revenue from advertisers who were willing to pay high CPMs for ads on our website.

For example, we might pay one cent for a click to our site via AdWords. That click to our site would result in maybe three or four impressions on the ads we ran. But those advertisers were paying us a higher rate for the impressions, bringing in around five cents for every penny invested in AdWords. It might not sound like a lot, but when you multiply it by tens of hundreds of thousands of clicks, you're talking about serious money!

We also used search engine marketing (SEM) to capture all the search volume for people looking to go out and buy tickets for big events like Halloween, New Year's, Valentine's Day, Thanksgiving, and more. These leads were very lucrative up until around 2009, when the rest of the industry caught on. But up until that point, we were paying pennies per lead, and leads would bring a profit, on average, of about a hundred dollars per ticket. It was like stealing candy from a baby and hitting the jackpot at the same time.

Eventually, as I've said, our costs rose significantly due to increased competition. However, because we had been running AdWords so long and Google had a history of our spends—we were easily spending up to $500,000 per year, which was a lot at that time—we were still able to run our ads profitably. Suffice it to say, JoonBug wasn't just about throwing parties and hoping to be discovered by the masses. We were a full-on marketing machine, a small team of smart people utilizing super-sophisticated online marketing tactics. Because of that, we completely dominated the most unlikely of offline verticals: nightlife and events!

Photo Finish

Today, taking pictures and posting them online is as easy as a few taps on your smartphone. But back in the early 2000s, it was a laborious, tedious task. The pictures produced by early cellphone cameras were notoriously pixelated, fuzzy, and bleak, spawning the goofy term "potato cam" (meaning you might as well use a potato to take pictures with). Decent digital cameras were available, but at a very steep price.

On top of the potato-cam and price problems, it was a huge pain in the neck trying to get the digital pictures off your device and onto a computer, where you could actually use them. When (and if) you did get them on your computer's hard drive, you had to go through all kinds of technological gymnastics to process the photos and display them.

But I was determined to make it work, and not just for one camera and one photographer; as we grew, JoonBug needed a system for processing and displaying photos from an army of photographers in different cities across the U.S., uploading tons of high-quality images with the fastest turnaround time possible.

A system that could handle all that? Nonexistent. This was a job for custom-built backend software, and I spent months building it out.

Post-It Notes

We had already committed to using high-end digital cameras, despite the cost. There was no question of using crappy cell-phone pictures in this arena. The first issue we had to resolve was how we could enable our remote team of photographers to upload their high-res digital photos. At the time, it seemed like the only option was having them physically drop off their memory cards so that we could do it for them on-site at our office.

That wouldn't do. I started work on a backend website for JoonBug.com that would allow our photographers to log in, using unique credentials, and then upload from their own computers. The logging in part was easy enough. But browsers back then didn't have the capabilities to streamline the uploading of mass numbers of photos. It's something that's taken for granted today, using Facebook or Snapfish or any other photo-friendly platform. But back then, it was a tough problem to solve, especially without native support for it in browsers, or open-source code you could copy and reuse.

So, we had to build our own Java applet to do the job. Although they're deprecated now, like Flash, at that time Java applets were basically the only way to do advanced tasks in browsers. The finished applet took weeks of debugging, cross-browser testing, and server-crashing before it was really up and running. We logged lots of hours on the phone, supporting our photographers as they navigated the process with us. But we finally got it down, and once it was all done, our photographers loved us! They were able to log on late at night or early in the morning after an event and have their photos uploaded in minutes.

This became another thing that made JoonBug stand out. We always had our photos ready to view within twelve hours of the event. People waiting to see their pictures were pleasantly surprised, even delighted, by the quality and the speed. We even created an email notification system that would alert patrons (after they gave us their email addresses, of course) when a particular event's photos were ready to view, so that those who couldn't wait would be able to see their pictures as soon as possible.

Talking Shift

The next challenge was coordinating the photographers' shifts for all the events we covered. This wasn't as difficult in the beginning, of course, but as time went on, there were sometimes up to forty events needing coverage on a given night, adding up to hundreds of events per week. That required us to have lots of standby freelance photographers available, some of them taking on two or three shifts each night (if the events were close to each other and had workable start and end times).

These photographers were all individual hires we found through Craigslist or word of mouth, the only viable ways of finding enough of them back then. We screened them by doing in-person interviews at our office or phone interviews if they were based in other cities. But for scheduling, there was once again no off-the-shelf solution that fit our needs, so we had to make one. It took another few months to develop and perfect, but it worked something like this:

1. We entered all our photographers into the system.
2. We entered all available shifts for a given week into the system.
3. The system would send an email alert to all the photographers, inviting them to sign in and pick up a shift.
4. Any shifts not picked up within six hours were emailed to us, so that we could get on the phone and figure out how to get them covered.

This way of doing things put most of the scheduling work in the hands of the photographers, rather than on the shoulders of our JoonBug staff. Before, handling the scheduling was a time-consuming pain in the neck, requiring tons of phone calls and emails spent trying to round up our photographers and get them penciled in. This way, the photographers could simply select the shifts that worked for them and keep moving.

Cheat Deterrent

After their shifts, photographers had to log in and upload. The photos went into a queue for manual review, so that we could make sure that the photographers were meeting our guidelines for the number of pictures, the image quality, and originality (not just snapping pictures from the same angle, or of the same people, over and over).

Later on, we discovered another issue we had to keep tabs on: photographers *not* actually showing up to the shifts they took, and instead uploading old pictures from the same venue taken weeks or months prior! We had to build in technology to check the file names they uploaded against prior uploads as a way of detecting duplicates. It wasn't a perfect algorithm, but it was better than nothing.

Still, I felt like we needed an extra layer of deterrent. Image recognition software was not something I could singlehandedly pull off, but the photographers didn't need to know that! We came up with the idea of warning all our photographers that we had the technology in place to catch any cheating, and I programmed a semi-fake progress bar to pop up while the photos uploaded, with an alert that read, "System checking for duplicates."

The backend system also helped us with generating reports and calculating payments every month. We could run the numbers on each photographer, how many shifts they had fulfilled and how much each shift was worth. Then we could simply cut the checks. It sounds simple, but as with scheduling, keeping track of it all manually had been a huge time-suck.

No Freebies

Once the photos were uploaded, reviewed, and posted to the site, anyone could view them—with a catch. The deal was that anyone who visited JoonBug.com, registered or not, could see small thumbnails of the photos. But when they clicked to enlarge an image, they would be prompted to register or log in first.

However, we quickly realized that most people were getting around that, by right-clicking and downloading the image through their browser. Then they could see the images full-size, and even email them to friends!

We had to outsmart the people outsmarting us, and that was another time my advanced programming skills came in handy. The answer was once again in the form of an applet. I made one to display the image when clicked, and dynamically add a JoonBug logo watermark to the lower-right corner. This killed two birds with one stone. Much to the frustration of most people, right-clicking the thumbnail was now useless. There was no way to download the image because it wasn't actually an image anymore—it was an applet! And for those technically savvy enough back then to take screenshots (which wasn't a built-in function in most operating systems), we were still covered. The watermark would at least spread the JoonBug brand to whoever saw the pictures.

Sharing is Caring

The finishing touch to our photo workflow was novel back then, but ubiquitous today: a "share" button. Before sites like Facebook were even a thing, we placed a share button underneath our photos, which allowed users to email a copy of the picture to their friends.

Recipients of the emailed copy, naturally, had to register to see the photo. That small button was a big winner for us, in terms of viral sharing and discovery. Grassroots sharing of our photos earned us a flood of new contacts in our database.

Prints Charming

After realizing that they could no longer download our images, a lot of subscribers started calling and emailing to see if we would sell them the originals or prints without watermarks. That sent me on a chase to figure out how we could make that happen. Selling them the digital file was simple. The hard part was figuring out how to provide good-quality prints.

Back then, Snapfish and similar sites were just getting started, and they were clunky, obscure, and unresponsive. I tried contacting them, but with no luck. They wouldn't email me back and didn't even have a phone number I could call.

I also looked into getting our own digital photo printer, but those were enormously expensive, difficult to operate, and slow. Who would want to sit there every day, manually loading photos onto a drive, printing them, stuffing them into envelopes, and shipping them? That would be a whole separate business, and one that we didn't want to get into. No, what I envisioned was a simple way that users could order prints right off our website, and have them printed, packed, and shipped with maximum quality and efficiency.

As luck would have it, around that time one of my younger cousins went to a prom and sent me some photo samples from the photographer's website. I noticed that there was an option to purchase prints through the website, and I was stunned! How could this photographer, running a small-time mom-and-pop business, know how to get this done, when I couldn't figure it out even after all my weeks of research and phone calls? I had to know how he was doing it, so I started to reverse-engineer his website, looking for clues in the HTML.

Within an hour, I struck gold. Hidden amongst the lines of code was a reference to another website, called Print Masters. It was a bit tricky, but I figured out that that part of his website was actually a white label (also known as private label) of the Print Masters website.

White labeling allows you to use the website or technology of another company and customize it with your own header, footer, colors, logos, and even a custom URL. It looks like the whole thing is your own site, and the end-user wouldn't know any different. I knew all about this from my time at Convey.com. Just like Medium now, Convey.com was a prime example of white-labeling. Users could create blogs that looked like they were unique to the bloggers, even though they were actually powered by our platform.

I found the Print Masters phone number and gave them a call. I couldn't believe what I was hearing! The guy on the other end of the phone was describing my ideal scenario: they could either white label the software, or we could handle our own purchases and send them batches nightly for printing and shipping. They also offered custom packaging with our logo, and whatever inserts we wanted to put in the envelopes! It was an incredible deal.

High-Flying Flywheel

I had miraculously stumbled upon the perfect solution to our problem, and we set it up within a week. We placed a "Buy Prints" button next to each photo on the site, sent out an email blast to advertise the new feature, and were selling like crazy in no time.

It all worked seamlessly. Each night, we put together a batch order for printing and sent it off to Print Masters. Eventually, we did include special inserts along with the prints, mostly flyers and coupons advertising our upcoming events. Print Masters charged us flat rate shipping for each package, and somewhere between five and twenty-five cents for a standard 4x6 print, depending on the volume of prints we ordered in a given month. If we needed or wanted other sizes, they had great prices on those, as well.

What was kind of unbelievable was the price we were able to charge! When I was checking out the prom photographer's website, I noticed that his prices for prints started at about fifteen bucks, which was a shockingly high number, in my opinion. But I figured if he was doing it and staying in business, then perhaps people would pay that much for our prints, too. Worst case scenario, we could lower our prices. It's easy to lower them, but very difficult to raise them, so it made sense to start out high.

We charged $15 per print, and unbelievably, none of our customers seemed deterred or put off by that price. We had no complaints and tons of orders. We also started selling the original, high-resolution digital version without the watermark, for twenty-five bucks. With those, customers could go to any print shop or pharmacy and order their own prints.

Soon it became clear that we were making enough money from selling prints to start sending more photographers to more events. Print sales would cover the costs and then some. And that's exactly what we did. We doubled the number of events we photographed, and it didn't cost a dime. As a result, JoonBug doubled the amount of data we collected each and every day from people registering to see and purchase their photos!

It was a quintessential example of a flywheel business, with each part of the business feeding into the next, creating more and more momentum. Event hosts and venues wanted the exposure of their event photos on our website; patrons wanted to see their photos the next day and, in many cases, purchase them; photographers wanted to pick up shifts and get paid; and we wanted to get as much data as we could, as fast as possible, at minimal marginal costs. Once we had the data, we monetized it through ads and ticket sales, and the cycle started again.

Pictures are worth a thousand words, but in our case, they were worth millions of dollars, and became one of the main components driving our business engine.

Check Your Inbox

As I've mentioned several times already, email was an integral tool that JoonBug used to monetize our subscribers. We sent out emails constantly, whether our dedicated email blasts, The Weekly Buzz newsletter, birthday promotions, or the crazy numbers of emails sent when users shared photos and event listings from our site. Unlike now, when there are plenty of email service providers with all the bells and whistles, they were virtually nonexistent when we started JoonBug. And so, you guessed it: we built one ourselves.

The Office Pet

In the beginning, when our database was relatively small, I made a barebones email system, using my own desktop computer as an email server. That meant hacking the computer to install an SMTP (Simple Mail Transport Protocol), and then writing my own custom Python scripts to query the database and send the emails each day. It took anywhere between three and ten hours to send the emails, once I had the script ready. The upside was that it worked, and it was free. The downside was that the process was super taxing on my computer, slowing it down to a crawl that tested my nerves and erased my productivity.

I graduated from using my desktop as a server to buying an out-of-the-box SMTP email and web server device, called a Cobalt Qube. It was a real and powerful server, but small enough to fit on my desk—a quirky little box with rounded edges in an appealing blue color. That little box carried the burden of our increasingly massive email marketing campaigns for the next six months.

The Qube was a lifesaver for us. First of all, because it took a load off my personal computer, so I could finally work! Second, it was able to send out emails at a much more rapid pace than my clunky Windows desktop, because the Qube was optimized for that specific task, running on a Linux OS and specialized hardware that were both very fast.

At the time, the JoonBug office was a seventy-five-square-foot room that just barely held our two desks, facing each other. Ariana and I had rented the space as a sublease, part of a larger office in the WeWork style. We had our little office, and other businesses rented the other rooms in the building, with everyone sharing the common areas and facilities.

The Qube had a lot of personality, as some office machines do, and it quickly became an odd but important member of our office family. While Ariana and I carried on the day-to-day operations of the business, the Cobalt Qube was like the little engine that could, chugging away at sending emails. When not in use, it would sit quietly, occasionally emitting a little quacking chirp. But when I initiated an email blast, a green light on the front panel would flicker and glow, and the Qube's CPU would go into a quacking frenzy, churning out all those emails.

That quack, fast or slow, permeated the whole room all day. The Qube was our fellow worker, our office pet, our faithful duck-server working diligently to send out our emails as fast as it could.

Movin' On Up

Despite its cuteness, the Qube was worn out and ready for retirement once we hit campaigns blasting out over 200,000 emails apiece. For my part, I couldn't keep writing custom scripts day after day, because it just wasn't scalable. We now had a chief marketing officer and other personnel who were responsible for updating the website, creating emails, and sending them out. The team needed an easy-to-use tool that would allow them to create emails in a WYSIWYG editor, choose the segments of our database to receive those emails, and schedule the emails to go out at specific times. The emails couldn't take hours or days to go out anymore. Most of them were now time-sensitive, sometimes having to be created and sent from start to finish in under forty-eight hours.

Enough time had passed that the available software options had evolved. I ended up using, and heavily customizing, Campaign Enterprise by Arial Software. We were one of their first customers, and they even did a case study on how JoonBug put their software to use. Although Campaign Enterprise was a good solution in terms of allowing our employees to carry out our email campaigns quickly and easily, it wasn't an SMTP server, so it was only one part of the equation.

I still had to find a serious upgrade to the Cobalt Qube, and the answer was purchasing several IronPort email servers. (Since then, Cisco has bought them and turned them into security appliances.) As the name suggested, IronPorts were the sturdiest option around, not only in terms of performance, but also in terms of sheer size and weight. They were huge, made with heavy-duty aluminum casings, and cost about $25,000 each. I bought two.

It was a major investment, but one we badly needed. Along with the servers, I had to purchase a whole rack system for installing them—the kind you see in commercial data centers. By then, we had moved into a proper 4,000-square-foot office down the street from our old two-person room, so we had a bit of extra space to put it all in. We also had access to the latest, fastest internet connection available, called a T3 line. It was super expensive, but blazingly fast compared to the other options at the time.

It took me about three weeks of long days and nights to finally configure both servers to work with Campaign Manager, but once I was done, it was like we had injected nitrous into our email engine! When we tested our first campaign on the new system, I limited it to 25,000 recipients, and three minutes after I pressed "Send," it said the process was complete. I thought that had to have been a mistake, so I spent the next several hours scouring the server logs, double- and triple-checking to make sure it had indeed gone out. Unbelievably, it was true: the system really was that fast.

The new servers even came with some built-in features that later proved game-changing, preventing us from getting caught in spam filters. For example, there was a "throttling" feature for particular domains that restricted us from sending emails to hotmail.com or yahoo.com addresses faster than five or six per second. Since the system was so fast, that was actually very important. Those email providers flagged any emails sent at high volumes and speeds, so purposely slowing the system down made it possible for our emails to get through to our customers' inboxes.

Our email game had turned into an extremely sophisticated setup for the time, unrivaled even by large enterprises. Compared to our competition in nightlife, it was unimaginably complex and advanced; lots of them still weren't doing email marketing at all. For us, it was worth every penny of the investment, setting us apart and putting us miles ahead of the competition.

New Tech > Old Tech (Sometimes)

When it came to selling tickets, JoonBug already had software that would keep an inventory of the tickets we sold and assign ticket numbers to each order. I had built it from scratch, and it was super effective. All you had to do was push a button, and the software did the rest, printing a receipt with the event, ticket numbers, and other relevant info. It auto-generated shipping labels as well if the user chose shipping instead of pickup. Back then, this was cutting-edge technology, although these days it's par for the course.

But by 2008, it was clear that JoonBug needed a new ticketing system, one that would use electronic delivery.

Smarter, Not Harder

To fulfill physical ticket orders, our team would print the precise number of physical tickets it took to sell out each event. Each ticket had a number and a foil seal, to make it hard to counterfeit. Then we would stay up all hours of the night in the office, processing the tickets. Pickup orders had to be placed into envelopes with the purchaser's name and filed alphabetically for easy retrieval. Shipping orders had to be sealed in envelopes and have the correct label applied.

It seemed that no matter how many temps we hired, it was never enough. Everyone, including Ariana and I, had to put in ridiculous hours to get the tickets out. (By that time, she and I were so good at it that we were each equivalent to about five temps in terms of output. That was a skill I didn't foresee mastering when we started out.)

I Think I Scan

Those endless nights, and the endless complaints that came with them, were the catalyst for my decision to create an e-ticketing system. I wanted customers to be able to receive their tickets by email and print them out at home. To make that work, each ticket would have a barcode to scan, in place of the former foil seal and ticket number. Our staff could use handheld barcode scanners to process the tickets at the door.

This new system would solve many of the issues we commonly faced with physical tickets, including:

- **Lost Tickets.** Occasionally, customers would call our office and say that their tickets had gotten lost in the mail. But from our end, there was no way to tell where the tickets had gone, or if a would-be patron was lying about the situation. With email, we wouldn't have to worry about re-shipping lost tickets or having duplicates out there, since each one had a unique code that could simply be canceled.
- **Shipping Costs.** E-tickets would allow us to eliminate shipping costs, which everyone hated to pay anyway. It was a real and frustrating pain point for our customers and avoiding it altogether would make transactions much more frictionless. (Eventually, a lot of customers would buy tickets from us for events that weren't even ours, just because our tickets were electronic and easier to get. It was odd, however, that although people hated paying shipping costs, they didn't flinch at our $3 convenience fee per e-ticket. For orders with multiple tickets, the convenience fees often added up to more than shipping would have! Who knows what the psychology of it was, but in the end, e-ticket convenience fees would also make us a lot of money. We kept the extra three bucks per ticket and didn't have to pay FedEx or any other carrier. And when you're selling hundreds of thousands of tickets, that adds up!)
- **Time and Personnel.** As I've said, the late nights and extra staff spurred me to create the new system. And once we implemented it, I was sure we would eliminate the need to put in long hours and hire extra people to fulfill orders. We could spend more of our time doing parties and other stuff that would grow the business—and more time sleeping! It was a cost-saving measure and a huge time-saver, too.

- **Scammers.** JoonBug often had to deal with people making their own fake tickets and trying to get into our events. But barcode-stamped e-tickets would virtually eliminate any fraud, because when we scanned each ticket, we'd immediately know if it was authentic or not—and each barcode could only be used once for entry. Trying to reverse-engineer a barcode system would take a Ph.D. in computer science, not to mention the costs involved. It really wouldn't be worth anyone's time to bother faking it.

Getting to Work

Building out the system took about six months of incessant work and plenty of money. Just finding the scanner hardware turned out to be extremely difficult and time-consuming. Nowadays, you can just search Amazon or Alibaba for these kinds of devices. But back then, you had to find a distributor and deal with their sales team (who really didn't know much about anything and would say anything you wanted to hear to make the sale).

I ended up ordering samples from various places and spent hours and hours trying to figure out if the devices they sent would even work with the system we had. Barcode scanners were, as you might guess, super-expensive at that time. Each handset could cost upward of five grand! If you're doing almost fifty events per night, with each event needing two to four scanners, that comes out to a lot of dough!

And of course, programming everything was incredibly costly and tedious as well. I was basically creating a whole new technological approach to automating a very complex process, a methodology that would be used day in and day out across innumerable events, operators, and tickets. All of this from scratch. But we were willing to make the investment, and if it worked, it would *still* end up being cheaper and more efficient than dealing with physical tickets.

An EZ Choice

The ultimate example of building what you can't buy was EZ Texting, a brand-new business born out of JoonBug's need to send text messages to our database.

In late 2005, we were humming along, busily managing all the moving parts involved with our events, photos, and website. But our email campaigns were beginning to suffer. The problem was "email fatigue."

In the beginning of our foray into email, we were the only game in town (and in your inbox). By 2005, though, with the rise of ESPs such as Constant Contact and Mailchimp, everyone and their mother had an email list going. That meant that our subscribers were getting nightlife emails not only from JoonBug, but also from the clubs they went to, the promoters they knew, and the brands they liked.

JoonBug became just another one of the 3,453,623 marketing emails flooding everyone's inboxes, which posed a whole new problem for us. Before, the issue was getting emails out as fast and efficiently as possible. Now, we had to figure out a way to cut through the clutter. The efficacy of our email blasts was diminishing rapidly, and the problem was only getting worse as more and more businesses tried to get their piece of the email-marketing pie.

Around the same time, texting started moving into the mainstream in the U.S. I think that this development was mainly due to the rising popularity of Blackberries, with their famously text-friendly QWERTY keyboards. Texting was already big in Europe and Asia, and the U.S. was starting to catch on with greater enthusiasm.

It seemed obvious to me, taking stock of these two trends, that the only way we could possibly survive the email apocalypse was by taking advantage of texting. But once again, the same old problem reared its head. There was no platform available that would allow us to utilize texting for our purposes! However, I had figured out the email problem, and I was determined to find or build the tech I needed for texting, too.

First, I tried to find a solution I could use, hack, or customize, spending almost two weeks searching around. I needed software that would allow JoonBug to send mass text messages to our existing database. But there was nothing! The difference between texts and email is that you can't just send texts via the internet. It requires special connectivity into the carrier phone systems to do it. I did find a few services that offered just what I needed, but they were only for Europe, Australia, and parts of Asia.

After digging around for another few weeks, I finally discovered a company called MX Telecom, based out of the UK, that specialized in SMS communications and—this is the key point—somehow had a 212 phone number listed on their website. 212 is the coveted, original NYC area code. It seemed impossible, but I called anyway.

A guy named Aly answered, and he didn't have a British accent, so that was a start. I asked him a few questions about their service, and if they might be able to help me with texts in the U.S. He answered positively.

"We just launched our service here in the U.S. two weeks ago," he explained. "I was hired to head up our operations in North America, so yes. We can definitely help you."

It was too good to be true, and I was jumping up and down inside! Again, it seemed that I'd hit the jackpot. I asked him where their office was located, and he said they were on the corner of 20th and 6th Avenue. That was literally a block away from where I stood at my desk! I will never forget that moment. "Are you in the office right now?" I asked.

"Yeah, I'm here now."

"I'm going to be there in five minutes to speak with you in person. Is that all right?"

"Well, yeah, sure! Come on over."

I hung up the phone and, without further ado, ran—literally—over to their office.

Once I got there, Aly filled me in on how the world of business SMS in the U.S. worked, and all about short codes (text-specific numbers assigned to businesses, as in "Text 12345 for more deals"). He said he could get JoonBug a short code, and not only that, he also could help me get it provisioned and connected to each of the cell phone carriers in the U.S. It would be, he warned me, a complex, expensive, and time-consuming process, taking about three months to get approved on all carriers. But to me, that was actually a blessing: if it took that much time and work to get going, then the whole thing was probably out of reach for most of our competitors!

In any case, I filled out all the necessary forms and got Aly a check that same day. For our short code, I settled on 25827, which spelled out the word "CLUBS" on a cellphone keypad. Because it was a vanity short code, the cost to lease it was a thousand dollars per month instead of the standard five hundred. And that didn't include setup costs (around ten grand) and monthly connectivity charges (three grand). Finally, there were the charges incurred per text sent and received.

It wasn't cheap, that was for sure. But I didn't care because I knew it would be worth it! I decided to call the new project "Club Texting."

Once we got the ball rolling with the short code and connectivity, the next step was to create the software we needed to send and receive mass texts from our database. I spent the next several months working on that, and the beta version was just about done by the time our short code was fully provisioned on all carriers.

The software itself was rudimentary at best, with an ugly, minimal-in-a-bad-way UI. When you logged in, all you could do was choose from a few basic options: upload a new list of contacts, send a text message, check your inbox, or set up a keyword. Of course, there was more going on behind the scenes.

One thing we needed was an unsubscribe option, so the software was programmed to search for words like "Stop" or "Cancel" and unsubscribe users with a follow-up confirmation text.

A more interesting aspect of the software was the keyword option. It allowed users to text a special word to our short code to join a list or take advantage of a promotion. You've probably seen this kind of call to action before—for example, texting the word "free" to a business's short code to get a freebie or coupon from them. (Bed Bath & Beyond loves to use these promotions.)

Once you text the keyword in, they capture your phone number, subscribe you to a list, and send you an auto-response with a link for a downloadable coupon. That's exactly what our software did: set up keywords users could text in, sent a customized, 160-character auto-response, and subscribed the user to a selected list. The software also allowed us to simply type out a text and send it to a list or group of lists, and in about five minutes, the text would blast to all of those phone numbers virtually simultaneously.

When it was finally time to put the software to the test, I imported a large segment of about 50,000 people from our database into the system and typed out the first text. It took me about an hour, with the help of three other people at JoonBug, to craft the perfect first message. It was for our Halloween event at a club in Tribeca called Flow, which we were doing for the first time that year. I don't remember exactly what we wrote, but it was something to the effect of:

JoonBug: Boo! Halloween is creeping up, so don't be a ghoul! Get your party tickets now! [Link]

With the text composed and typed into the software's input form, I stood there nervously, my finger hovering over the send button. What if the software didn't work? What if there was some kind of a bug that I didn't catch? Once I pressed send, there was no going back. What if it spiraled into an endless loop, texting fifty thousand of our subscribers over and over into oblivion?

At least five minutes passed while I stood there, frozen, but finally I gathered my courage and hit "send." The browser submitted, the software went to work, and I sat there with my heart pounding, waiting for the confirmation page to render. It took about two minutes (give or take an eternity) for it to finish, but finally, the page popped up with the simple, bland confirmation statement I had programmed into it: "Your text was sent."

Of course, I wasn't really sure that all of the texts had gone through successfully, so to check, I clicked over to the inbox. There were already hundreds of responses in there, with more popping up every second. People were texting back things like, "how much," "What time?" and more— and of course there were a fair number that said "stop texting me" or some variation thereof. But the amazing thing was just the *volume* of immediate responses.

We could never have gotten that level of response via email, even at our most successful.

So, sharing a single login to the basic HTML interface I'd coded, my employee Josh and I jumped in and started frantically texting everyone back, having conversations with them, and selling them on parties through text (which was much easier than over the phone!). It was a complete paradigm shift, and I knew that not only would we love it for its amazing results, but that our subscribers would love it too, because it was so easy. Texting in short, easy-to-understand, asynchronous messages was much more pleasant than dealing with calls and much more effective than sifting through an overflowing inbox.

Within twenty minutes, we had sold about fifty tickets, just from that one text message. It was explosive, completely unlike the slow trickle of email responses we were used to. By the end of the day, the number of orders exceeded one hundred, an ROI that was absolutely insane! It seemed that we had hit digital gold, and I was ready to send out our next text blast immediately, so that we could continue to capitalize on our success.

Message Envy

Later on that day, my phone blew up. About twenty different promoters called as the afternoon went on, all of them asking me how I sent out that message. They had gotten the text too, because so many people in the nightlife industry had registered on our website. They all wanted to know how I had done it, what service I was using, what the short phone number was about, and much more. Lots of them had long lists of phone numbers they wanted to target, and it was too costly and time-consuming to call the normal way.

To the first few guys who called me, I answered that it was an internal system that I had built for JoonBug. But this got the wheels turning in my head, and I thought to myself, "Well, if these guys need it, perhaps I should offer it to them for a fee ... it would lower our costs of running the software and leasing the short code ..."

So, when the next person called, I told them it was a service JoonBug had started. "It's called Club Texting, and it's in stealth beta mode right now. If you're interested, I can put you on the waitlist?"

It felt so ironic, because I was actually using the same psychology on these promoters that they used on patrons all the time: making them feel special for gaining "exclusive access" to what was, more or less, a "VIP area" in marketing!

They fell for it harder than a desperate guy waiting all night outside the hottest club, hoping there was even a fraction of a chance that the doorman would let him inside. "Wait list?" one guy bellowed into the phone. "I'm gonna be your biggest customer! I'm not a waiter, I don't wanna wait—how much does it cost? I'll pay double—" and on and on. All of them were throwing their weight around like would-be bottle buyers trying to fake their way into a club with their machismo, status, and wallet!

For my part, I was making it all up on the fly. My "stealth beta waitlist" consisted of a hastily thrown-together spreadsheet of all the people who had called wanting to sign up. It reached around twenty-five names by the end of the day, all of whom became paying customers as soon as I got them into the system. Since everyone was asking what it cost, I had to come up with pricing, quick. Our cost per text was about half a penny. I multiplied that by a hundred to get five cents per text. And although I thought that was a pretty steep markup, no one else batted an eye, because the standard rate for text messages back then was ten cents. It must have sounded reasonable to them—especially compared to spending hours and hours manually texting everyone on your list at double the price per text.

Sharing Is Caring (and Profitable)

I spent the next two weeks making a multi-user version of the software, so that other promoters, clubs, and brands could log in and use it.

The first month of Club Texting was a pleasant whirlwind. The clients were logging in, uploading their lists, and setting up keywords, while I helped them with technical issues, bug fixes, and learning the software. I was having a great time. It felt fantastic to be back in the business of building something that other people could use and benefit from.

I had added a $100 monthly minimum spend, with no rollover, and we had around forty signups that first month. It was a good start, sure, but I didn't think much of it, because in my mind, that only represented forty people spending a hundred dollars each. My only thought was that it would help to subsidize the cost of leasing the short code, paying for connectivity, and so on.

But when the end of the month came along, and it was time to bill everyone, the total came to just about $20,000. We were bringing in about $10,000 in pure profit!

Some of our customers were sticking to their limit of around a hundred bucks, as I had anticipated, but there were a bunch of them spending between four and five hundred, and still others racking up thousands of dollars' worth of texts.

That moment was like a beacon, flashing an unmistakable signal: "Wake up, dummy! This is a big opportunity!"

I had a very clear vision of what I had to do next. It was clear that I had to take the Club Texting project to the next level, and for the next several months, I spent every waking moment doing so.

Within a year, Club Texting had evolved into EZ Texting, with around 1,000 customers from a number of different industries, generating over half a million in revenue. A small side project, originally designed to help JoonBug cut through the clutter of mass email, had become a full-fledged, highly successful SaaS company.

Nightlife Lessons Learned

Running a business is about providing a product or service that people need or want. But along the way, it's almost a given that you'll discover ways to automate, enhance, and allow greater productivity, efficiency, volume, or value.

Maybe the right tool already exists, or maybe you'll have to get your hands dirty and build it yourself. Either way, having the technical understanding to evaluate the situation is crucial. If you have that knowledge base, or at least if you're willing to acquire it, you'll be light-years ahead of most of your competition.

And as you troubleshoot, source, and build, you may just find that you've uncovered new opportunities for even greater success.

The lesson here is fairly simple. If you need something, other people will likely need it too. So, if it doesn't exist, build it! Suddenly, you've made a product or service to sell that may well become a new business (that could even surpass your existing business).

I've seen a number of examples of this while in the venture capital business. Probably the best-known one is Slack. It was an internal communications tool developed at a company that built online games, but it worked so well that it became the new focus of the company.

That's more or less what happened with EZ Texting as well. Once we released it, the business really took off, and it soon became a rival with JoonBug for my time, energy, and passion, as well as an even more profitable venture. I had loved working with JoonBug in the NYC nightclub scene, yet the all-nighters every night were starting to take their toll, and, in my mid-thirties, I was beginning to seek something different. But that's a story for another (night) life lesson.

EVERYBODY LOVES YOU ... FOR THE RIGHT PRICE

MONEY TALKS. THAT'S JUST A fact. And oftentimes, money is all it takes to turn your biggest critic into your biggest fan.

It was a cycle that I became familiar with—fast. Starting out, a lot of club owners and promoters despised JoonBug, because we were "too mainstream." They talked a lot of trash about us, sometimes about me and Ariana personally, even to our faces.

Ego-tripping on their fifteen minutes of nightlife fame, owners of popular hotspots would brag that they weren't in it for the money. (This was good because they were usually broke.) Instead, they loftily claimed to be connoisseurs of the world of nightclubbing, curating crowds and "crafting unforgettable experiences."

But we didn't care what they said, because we knew that the tide would always turn. Every club and promoter would have an event they were desperate to pack out. And in those cases, they only had one sure way: JoonBug. We were always on the receiving end of frantic calls about setting up promotions or sending out email blasts, and that's when we would take full advantage of the situation, charging double or triple our normal rate.

It was a taste of sweet revenge, with a side of cold hard cash. Yes, we made them pay through the nose, but we also provided excellent service, and the owners who worked with us always ended up making a great profit. Our brand was the most important thing to us, so we worked hard to deliver an outstanding result every time.

The vindication we felt was laughably predictable: all it took was a big fat paycheck from a successful event, and the guys who had previously despised us as too uncool, mainstream, or even stupid, were now magically our best pals. They couldn't get enough of us. So much for not being in it for the money!

The Capitale Affair

A case in point is a Halloween party we did for Capitale one year. We had already thrown a Halloween party for them the year before, which had been super successful, selling over 6,000 tickets and leaving everyone (including ourselves, frankly) amazed.

What we didn't know at the time was when promoters notice a certain venue having success, they often laser focus on that venue, hoping to cash in. Using whatever leverage they have there, as buddies with the owner or friends of friends, they try to get in on other people's success and land a deal to manage the next big event there. If they can secure the venue, they will then hire sub-promoters to do all the work, while they sit back and let the money roll in. Sometimes these guys would even hire JoonBug to advertise or sell tickets. Ariana and I found ourselves in a constant tooth-and-nail fight not to let that happen, and our first battle was with Richie Akiva and Scott Sartiano of Butter Group.

No Honor Among Promoters

Richie and Scott saw our success with the Capitale Halloween party, and since they were great friends with Capitale's owner, Seth Greenberg, they tried to convince him to let Butter Group do the following year's Halloween. They put a lot of pressure on him. For his part, Seth was somewhat torn and ended up telling me and Ariana about the situation.

We blew a gasket, pointing out how much money we'd made for him, not just at Halloween, but on New Year's Eve and Thanksgiving Eve as well! But Seth wasn't hearing us. When your venue is hot, your ego is through the roof, and you think it will last forever. Plus, Butter Group had promised to bring Jay-Z and his whole crew to Capitale for Halloween, if Seth gave them the event. They were speaking Seth's language of prestige, celebrity, notoriety, and fame. Ariana and I were talking dollars and cents, which should have carried more weight but it didn't. We threatened to back out of all the other parties we had planned there, but even that didn't resonate.

Joon...Butter?

Negotiations weren't going anywhere, and eventually I realized that the only thing I could do was swallow my ego and change tactics.

Instead of trying to oust Butter Group, we proposed a different plan: collaborating with them. Seth agreed to make that partnership happen, but no one was very happy about it.

We set up a meeting, and right out of the gate, Scott and Richie refused to show, pretending to be too cool and "busy" to bother planning the actual event. Instead, they sent their minions, Mike Heller and Jeffrey Goldstein. These two seemed like an odd choice of right-hand-men: Mike's dad was an attorney, famous for representing big names like Mariah Carey; Mike himself was also an attorney, moderately well-known for having a famous dad. As for Jeffrey Goldstein, he was just sort of along for the ride. His day job was as owner of a clothing boutique in the Hamptons.

Nevertheless, they were our contacts with Butter Group, and we all sat down together one afternoon to plan out the party. I don't think Mike and Jeffrey had worked with promoters who were professional, or even organized, before. Lots of promoters back then didn't have a strategic or detail-oriented approach to planning. Events were often slapped together at random, with the people involved hoping rather than planning for success.

But JoonBug was different, and purposely so. Again, we were playing a long game, so Ariana and I treated everything in a businesslike manner and were detail-oriented to a fault. We came prepared, ready to hammer out a master plan, including the schedule for the evening, necessary security, DJ (and backup DJs), graphic design for the invites, and everything else.

Mike and Jeffrey weren't so prepared, but for their contribution to our planning session, they revealed that they'd lined up the Gastineau Girls to host the party. The Gastineau Girls were a pseudo-celebrity mom and daughter team, starring in their own reality TV show before the reality-TV-bubble burst. The show had pushed them a grade or two above their normal B-list, NYC-socialite status. As they were going to be the party's "hosts" for the evening, we were supposed to put their photos and names on the invites.

Which brought Mike and Jeffrey to their next point. Butter Group had one very specific and important demand: top billing. They informed us that we should design the invites with Richie and Scott's names at the top, followed by Mike and Jeffrey's names, and finally JoonBug in third place.

Considering how much of the actual planning was being done by JoonBug, this was utter garbage. But Ariana and I went along with it—at least in the meeting. When it came time to have the actual invitations made, we went ahead and put the JoonBug logo right at the top where it belonged. The Butter Group guys had a cow when they saw the printed invites, but it was too late. We blamed it on a mistake with our designer. "Oops!"

Selling Out (In a Good Way)

Once everything was planned out, Ariana and I put the party plans through the JoonBug machine. The invites were made, and we organized the email blast accordingly, along with the posting on our site. Everything went off without a hitch, and within about a week, nearly all of the thousands of tickets were sold. The Butter team was in shock.

But we didn't stop there. Ariana and I came up with another way to sell even more tickets: offering discounted "after midnight" entry. The idea was that about half the crowd usually leaves at around midnight anyway, so at that point, admitting more patrons would work out fine. We sold after-midnight tickets at a tempting sale price, and it went very well. In fact, it became one of our most lucrative tactics for optimizing events going forward.

Massive Masses!

The party was a madhouse. Before the doors even opened, there was a line wrapping around the block twice to get in. But it wasn't a tough wait; the weather was unusually warm for late October, and the crowd was its own entertainment, with everyone in costume. There was no shortage of pretty women in daring outfits and men checking them out. As usual with big events, Ariana and I were out with the door people and security, working hard to get everyone in as quickly as possible. It was doable but always a challenge.

Suddenly, a bunch of black SUVs with tinted windows pulled up right in front of the venue. There was a moment of collective realization, and then people started rushing and screaming toward the SUVs, while a storm of paparazzi flashbulbs lit up the scene. It was hard to tell just who was getting out of the vehicles, but as they made their way to the entrance, I saw more celebs in one minute than I had seen in my whole life up to that point! Jay-Z, Puff Daddy, Usher, Russell and Kimora Lee Simmons, Petra Nemcova, Lil' Kim, and Maya were following behind Scott Sartiano, who was personally escorting them to the club.

Honestly, Ariana and I were starstruck for a minute. We both just stood there, staring. Ariana snapped out of it first and went into action. "OK, all right," she yelled, striding in the direction of our security and directing them to clear a path for the celebrities and their entourage. A few moments later, I blinked, came back to reality, and radioed a photographer to come out there quick and capture all of this.

Scott was leading the group up to the VIP room, so Ariana and I went scurrying up the stairs to meet them there, as did their and some of our security. I remember the rush of excitement I felt as I jogged up those steps, thinking to myself that this night would set the stage for all our events going forward.

In the VIP area, all the other patrons stopped and stared as the group of celebrities entered and settled in. Puff Daddy and Jay Z whispered something in each other's ears, while the ladies eyed the decor. Scott sat down, and Ariana and I followed suit, smiling and greeting each person as Scott made the introductions. Then I surprised myself by blurting out, "Guys, let's take a photo to remember this Halloween." To my further surprise, they all easily agreed, posing for the camera with zero hesitation. And just like that, JoonBug became the owner of multiple incredible money shots, worth more than gold!

Check, Please

The day after the party, the JoonBug website struggled to keep up with all the traffic we were getting. I got warnings right and left from the server monitoring software, but thankfully the site didn't crash. Photos of the party made it to the press, as well; before we knew it, our event was the talk of the town.

As for money, when Ariana and I saw the total, we were in shock. Just in case, we did the math a few more times to make sure it wasn't some kind of mistake. The tickets, bar money, and cash from the door grossed almost $250,000 dollars.

We printed out a report and got a check ready for Mike and Jeff. When they showed up, they didn't even say hello. They just picked up the check, stared at it, and started laughing. Their cut was almost $125,000, and all they could do was hug us, kiss us, hug us some more, and ask if they were on some kind of reality prank show!

Next, they got Scott and Richie on the phone. As soon as those two heard about the check, they suddenly transformed from resentful and grudging co-promoters to our biggest fans. They gushed about how well everything had gone and babbled about the "next event" we could do together. They were even throwing around ideas about JoonBug doing events at Butter, which really showed how much they had changed their tune. Butter was arguably the most coveted venue in town, and Richie and Scott handled the promotions there exclusively; it was their special stomping grounds for wining and dining their VIP friends. In any other instance, the idea of having outsiders do promotions at Butter would have been sacrilege!

As for the report, none of them even glanced at it. They were used to working with scammers and con artists in the industry who couldn't be trusted to accurately account for expenses and profits, so they didn't bother checking the numbers. But Ariana and I always made a point of paying others first and ourselves last; we were building a reputation. Reputation is a priceless asset and kept us in the game long after the liars, cheaters, and scammers had come and gone.

Making It to Marquee

Both Ariana and I had been friendly with Noah Tepperberg and Jason Strauss for years before they opened Marquee. We'd even done a few parties for them, including the Suite 16 Thursdays (which had done better after that first failed night) and a memorable Thanksgiving event at Capitale, partnering with *Gotham* magazine. Noah and Jason were running that Capitale party and gave us 100 tickets to sell; we sold them all in one day. Then they gave us 500, and we sold those, too. After that, they wouldn't let us sell any more for the event, because they had to let the other promoters (and themselves) have their share!

Despite our history, we knew that JoonBug didn't have a shot of doing any parties at Marquee, at least in the first year. That was 2003. Although Marquee was situated in a crummy part of west Chelsea where nothing was going on, they had spent a good amount of money making the place beautiful, working with nightlife legend Steve Lewis on the design. It was thoughtfully and tastefully laid out, so much so that it became arguably the hottest club in NYC history.

Nobody had seen a club like that, and on top of it, they had Wass working the door. He always ran a tight ship and kept the crowd impeccably curated. Sometimes Ariana and I couldn't even get in! But we didn't take it personally. Besides, we knew that, like many other clubs, Marquee might not last. A lot of hotspots were nothing more than brilliant flashes in the pan. But if it did last, the prestige would wear off a little, and we would start doing events there.

We couldn't have been more wrong about the timelines. Marquee, as I've said, was extremely successful and nowhere near closing after the first year. Somehow, Noah and Jason had the magic touch, and Marquee was as hot the second year as it had been the first, and stayed that way into the third year, fourth year, and beyond. We tried to start booking events there, but no matter how much we called, asked, and even tried to bribe our way in (by offering to overpay to book Halloween and New Year's), it was always a no.

Things finally changed in early 2006, when JoonBug was hired to do an event for Trump Vodka and goTrump.com (a startup travel site riding on the Trump name). The celebrity high-profile nature of that event finally gave us the leverage we needed to get into Marquee. We called Jason and Noah personally and booked it with no problem.

The event was a great success. We had a red carpet and a backdrop with JoonBug logos and GoTrump logos. All kinds of celebrities came to celebrate, and Trump himself made an appearance. The press had a blast, and the place was absolutely packed out.

After that, we were a shoo-in with Marquee. By the following week we were negotiating contracts to book New Year's Eve there—at last! But a few days into the negotiation process, we hit a snag. The amount of money that they wanted was significant: too much, in fact, for us to actually turn a profit. The way we figured it, we'd barely break even. It was a major dilemma. We had worked so hard to get to that point, but now, losing the space and having to just walk away were a very real possibility.

I spent several sleepless nights talking it over with Ariana until we were blue in the face. Finally, we decided to bite the bullet and pay a whopping $300,000 for a venue that held only about 700 people, max—that's almost $500 per person. And not only that, we were taking on the financial burden of paying up front, even if we couldn't sell all the tickets—paying the DJ, door staff, security, marketing costs, and more.

Our thought process was that, first of all, if we didn't do it, someone else would! Plus, not only were our chances of selling out high, but there was also a real probability that there would be so much demand that we could push a lot of would-be patrons to our other, much more profitable New Year's Eve events.

We figured we would get some press out of it, and most importantly, our database would rack up all those high rollers who frequented Marquee. We would be able to market to them personally afterwards.

And finally, having the Marquee New Year's Eve event on our website would go a long way in the minds of other venue owners. With that kind of social proof, we'd be able to book spaces that we could never get otherwise. Again, owners and promoters are followers, not leaders, so if they saw that Marquee was doing something, they'd think, "We should be doing that too!"

So, we rolled the dice, and agreed to pay Marquee's insane booking price. And ... our plan worked perfectly.

Within a week, the event was sold out and even ended up making a profit. Our original estimates for how much we could charge were modest, and we were able to charge a lot more; plus, we sold a bunch of after-midnight tickets. Also, as we had hoped, we were able to push the overflow of patrons begging for tickets to some of our other events, selling those out.

As for press, we did get some coverage, although not in the way we had expected. The night of the party, Adam Duritz, the lead singer of Counting Crows, tried to get in without a ticket. I put my foot down, and in the end, he had to pay $1,000 cash to get in. That incident made it to Page Six the next day!

JoonBug did such a great job that night and made everyone so much money that we earned the respect and loyalty of all the guys from Marquee, and from many other venues as well. We were then able to book venues we'd never have had a shot at before. And for years to come, JoonBug did Halloween and New Year's for Marquee, even negotiating the booking price down to make it more profitable.

Raising Cain

Cain was one of the first "out of our league" venues we tried to book after Marquee. A few weeks after securing the Marquee deal and creating all the artwork and digital media for it, I picked up the phone and called Jamie Mulholland to ask if I could meet with him to discuss booking a private event at Cain. That was as specific as I wanted to get on the phone; I knew that if I asked to book New Year's Eve out of the gate, he would say no. He was already acting like he was doing me a favor, just by taking my call! So, I was as vague as possible, and insisted that it was a big event I needed to discuss with him in person.

For that meeting, I wore jeans, a white button-down, and a pale gray blazer. I had a contract in my hand, a check for $50,000, and a cheery demeanor. I wanted him to feel like this was a pleasant situation, that opportunity was knocking.

Seated in front of his desk, I thanked him for taking the time to meet with me. He eyed me cautiously and then asked in his South African accent, "So what can I do for you, mate?"

Without wasting words, I told him straight up that I wanted to book New Year's Eve and that I was willing to pay $100,000 for the room.

He looked at me for a second, and then laughed dismissively. "It's not about the money for me," he said loftily. I couldn't tell if he was really beginning to lose interest, or if it was just an act.

My next move was to slide the invite that I had made for Marquee across the table, telling him that we already had a contract in place with Marquee for New Year's Eve at that price. His eyes opened slightly, and I could see the gears turning in his mind. "I'm surprised you don't want to negotiate, given Marquee is doing it with us?" I said casually. "At a hundred grand, it would be a very profitable night for you."

He was silent, and I could see what was in his mind as clearly as if it were written on a billboard: "What do Jason and Noah know that I don't know?" For my final move, I pulled out the contract and the check, and put those on the table, as well. Now he was really shocked! It was visceral and real, and I had his full attention.

He looked at the check, the contract, and then at me, as if he were trying to decide whether to trust me or not. The tension held for only a moment before he relaxed and gave in. "You know, mate, I like you." He said with a grin. "I like your style. You're a smarty pants! Let's do this."

I left there with a signed contract in place and a big smile, full of confidence that we could pick off all the greatest places in NYC from here on out.

On New Year's Eve, Jamie arrived at Cain very concerned about the crowd we were bringing to his very exclusive venue. But when I dropped by on my rounds, I found him happy and relaxed. Whatever his fears had been about our party, they didn't come true; the crowd was great, upscale, and partying hard. Everyone was spending money and buying bottles, to the point that he started selling after-midnight tables to patrons trying to get in without tickets.

When I caught him doing that, I had to think fast. If I came at him aggressively, he wouldn't take it very well, and things could go south in a hurry. Instead, I approached him in a neutral manner. "Hey, I know this is your club. You can do whatever you want, and there's really nothing I can do to stop you. But we had an agreement, and it isn't right for you to sell tables when this is technically our event. We bought the venue from you for the night, so we should be selling the tables." I added that I did understand where he was coming from, though, and offered a compromise: we could just split whatever money was made from bringing in extra after-midnight patrons.

Again, his attitude changed from cautious to approving. He told me that I was "smart and dangerous," shook hands on the deal, and it was settled. We did a few shots at the bar to celebrate, and the next week I sent him a silver flask with the Cain logo and his name engraved on it. Honestly, we made him so much money that night that he should have been sending JoonBug gifts! But when he gave me a call to say thanks, I asked him to sign a multiyear contract with us for New Year's, and he couldn't say no.

And so, we went from being hated to being loved by another too-cool-for-school venue owner—just because we were that good at making them money.

The Things We Do for Love

All in all, having the hottest clubs on New Year's Eve, Halloween, and other big nights out was a great way to drive traffic and gain notoriety. But they weren't the real moneymakers, per se. In fact, the biggest moneymakers that JoonBug had often weren't clubs at all, and they certainly weren't exclusive. The ironic truth is that we made a ton of money working with the most mundane or overlooked places.

The key was demand. For example, JoonBug often got calls asking if parents could bring their kids along to this or that event, and eventually Ariana and I realized that there was a huge demand for family-style New Year's Eve parties, Halloween parties, you name it. We listened to those people and tried to show them some love by creating events tailored to their needs. One family-style event we would do was to rent out a venue like Dave and Buster's, create ticket categories for adults (18 and over) and kids (everyone under

18), and go from there. Those events were big hits, super profitable, and sold tickets like crazy.

Similarly, we put on events that native New Yorkers didn't care about at all—but out-of-towners did! Out-of-towners were prolific buyers of our New Year's Eve tickets at spaces that were considered uncool to any New York local. We could sell out Heartland Brewery on New Year's Eve, for example, because for tourists, the cachet of Times Square was synonymous with New Year's Eve. They couldn't be more excited to be in the middle of the action and potentially watch the ball drop live. And that remained true across numerous venues considered laughable by nightlife-industry elites. From the Hard Rock Cafe to Havana Central, tourists would pay top dollar for tickets to the events we created for them.

Creating multiple price points was important and helped us sell tickets in huge numbers to people who didn't necessarily want to drop $100 on a night out. We listened to those people, too, and came up with affordable, $25 ticketed NYE events. To offset costs on our end, we nixed the open bar and used affordable venues. Those events, too, were greatly loved (and by extension, so was JoonBug).

Having the best places? A facade. The real money came from any place that was cheap to rent out for a night but easy to pack with high-paying patrons. As I've explained before, exclusivity doesn't pay the bills, but by catering the masses, we were able to hit paydirt.

Love is Expensive

Our unique approach to creating events for the masses earned us plenty of money, but it also garnered us a lot of attention from other promoters. Because we were taking photos of everything and posting them very publicly on our website, it was obvious to anyone watching what we were up to. The JoonBug website became a way for other promoters to see how successful our events were at ordinary restaurants and spaces like Slate pool hall. And like clockwork, they copied us, competing for those venues the same way they would compete with us for Marquee or Cain. It would often lead to rather humorous situations, because no one (least of all the owners of the venues) was used to price wars over their neighborhood Olive Garden!

It had been hugely successful, but the price we had to pay to stay loved by our subscribers, sponsors, and venue owners got higher every year. It was what you might call inflationary love, which became increasingly unsustainable. When the price of love gets too high, it might be time to get out of the relationship … but that's a story for another lesson.

Nightlife Lessons Learned

People who are haters will always love you for the right price. Money buys happiness and money talks. The cool club owners/promoters might have hated JoonBug and thought we weren't "the cool crowd" or didn't have the right look. But we could populate their clubs with 500 to 1,000 people in minutes. Suddenly, the same guys who hated us became our best friends when they saw the lines out the door and the money rolling in at eleven p.m. Especially on New Year's Eve and Halloween, when their typical exclusive cool crowd was neither showing up nor paying.

When I started out as a real estate investor, it was the same story. The biggest real estate agents and owners looked down their noses when I would inquire about properties for sale. They weren't about to let me in on the best deals.

But once I had made them a lot of money with a couple of significant purchases, they accepted me with open arms as a major player and I became privy to top opportunities. Where before I would call people twenty times about a deal and never receive a return call, now they called me their new best friend.

LESSON 7

WHATEVER CAN GO WRONG, WILL GO WRONG

BEING AN ENTREPRENEUR IN THE events business is like firefighting. Your job is to constantly pivot, solve problems, do the best you can with what you have, and move on to the next job. Of course, unlike being a firefighter, you have to do it all while not breaking a sweat! Because if others see you freaking out, they'll freak out, too. That includes your employees as well as your patrons.

However, if you can act cool and collected, doing whatever you have to do to band-aid the situations that arise, most people will never notice, and the party will just keep going. Your brain might be running a thousand miles a minute, and your adrenaline might be pumping like crazy, but on the outside, you just have to keep smiling and playing it cool.

Murphy's Law for Nightlifers

JoonBug had to deal with a lot of issues, week in and week out, as we ran our business. Murphy's Law hit on an almost daily basis. While it was always challenging, we learned how to cope and how to avoid getting screwed too badly. Here are just a few of the problems we dealt with regularly.

No-Show DJs

This was such a constant problem that, at one point, I was contemplating learning to DJ myself, just to save time and money. Ultimately, we ended up keeping a few CDs ready in case of a no-show, and for big events, we hired not one, but two backup DJs!

Access Denied

Sending photographers all over the city to take professional photos was a key part of our business, but we quickly got used to getting calls at all hours of the night from panicked photographers, who had either gotten kicked out or were being refused admission to the club. The problem was usually some power-tripping manager, and it cost us hours of sleep-calling owners, promoters, and anyone else we could to get our guys past the velvet ropes. In the end, we learned to preempt this situation by having our assistants call everyone we knew at a problematic club a few hours before the evening began, just to make sure we were all on the same page about which photographer was coming and when.

Howdy, Sheriff

Sometimes, if one of our events was busy or maybe overpacked, the police or fire department would show up. Drunk people outside the club could cause a lot of noise, and neighbors would call the cops to settle things down. To mitigate that issue, we started hiring doormen who were off-duty cops, or event security with at least one retired or off-duty cop on staff. If anything went down, those guys had the experience to handle it without needing to bother the police.

Thinking On Our Feet

At other times, I had to think fast and react to things that were unforeseen and, in some cases, just outrageous. Nightlife has a way of attracting unusual characters, and the circumstances of a given party can be a perfect storm for chaos.

Too Many Whales

There was one event we did at Guastavino's when Frank and a few other whales showed up. This time, our whales spent so much on bottle service that by one in the morning, Guastavino's was literally out of booze! Several of us had to run out and jump into cabs and buses, hitting up liquor stores for magnums of Grey Goose and Dom Perignon. The party had to go on!

The Backdoor Scam

There were also instances in which club owners and venue managers saw how well a party was going and couldn't resist coming up with schemes to mess with JoonBug and get a cut of the action. A prime example was Capitale's general manager. At one of our New Year's events, she suddenly stopped the door, and when we asked why, she informed us that we had oversold the event, and Capitale was at capacity.

This was clearly not true. We were using our clicker to count tickets at the door, and we hadn't yet processed the number of tickets we'd sold, which were limited due to the club's size. We argued, but something had to give. It was ten o'clock at night, and there were tons of patrons outside in the cold, waiting. The manager made Ariana go inside and start counting ticket stubs to "prove" that we hadn't oversold.

But what was really happening was that the manager had the security guards lead patrons to the back entrance. Once they got there, the security guards would let them in—and pocket the money! We were being duped. This went on for about twenty minutes before the manager "came to her senses" and said we could start letting people in again.

At that point, one of our employees came and told us what had happened. I had never seen Ariana so furious before. She took it personally and went right up to a huge bouncer and started screaming for them to cough up the cash and give it to her. And they did! She confronted each security man, and it was an unbelievable sight. These huge, burly tough guys couldn't even look her in the eye and were obviously terrified down to their toenails of what she might do next!

A Bad Beat

There were also a few times when the security we hired allegedly beat someone up. If it happened, the person in question probably deserved it, frankly. But those incidents caused JoonBug to be dragged into a few civil lawsuits over the years. They were all eventually dismissed. We had insurance to cover the legal fees, and our security guys were hired as contractors, not employees, which protected us from liability. Nevertheless, lawsuits are a huge pain in the neck. Running a business is hectic enough without getting the courts involved!

At the end of the day, these kinds of issues were relatively benign. But there were two much larger incidents that were huge messes and resulted in very hard but valuable lessons learned.

A Cheat and a Check

After the demise of the legendary nightclub Au Bar, a well-known club owner and restaurateur named Stratis Morfogen brought it back to life. This time around, it was called Club 58. And one fateful day, JoonBug struck a deal with Morfogen to book it for New Year's Eve.

How to Book It

For the big nights like New Year's Eve and Halloween, we booked venues all over the city, including midtown, uptown, and Brooklyn. That way, we could cater to the broadest swath of patrons. Our booking with Club 58 didn't come cheap: we ponied up to the tune of $150,000.

When we booked venues, negotiations usually started five or six months in advance, and the main question was, of course, the overall price. To determine the number, we'd calculate things like an open bar with premium or house alcohol, a DJ (plus backups), staffing, security, a menu, the number of bottles per table, and various other things. Depending on the details, we would arrive at a price that made sense per person and then set the tab based on the maximum number of people we could expect.

Club 58 was a large venue, holding about 1,000 patrons, so even though the price was high, it made sense. We had never worked with Stratis before, but he seemed like a nice enough guy: put-together, charming, well-spoken, and very professional. Following the usual protocol, we put down a deposit of 10 percent to secure the venue and agreed to pay the balance a few days before the event.

In the meantime, we promoted the event and sold tickets. Again, this was a standard procedure for us; it helped with our cash flow because we didn't have to shell out millions of dollars all at once on venues before taking in cash from ticket sales.

A Tale of Two Payments

The Tuesday before New Year's, I sent a messenger to Club 58's office with a check for $135,000. The messenger service sent back the usual signed proof of receipt, and I didn't think any more about it—until Friday at noon. That was the day before the party, and that was the day I got a call from Stratis.

He was angry. Abruptly, he informed me that they had never received my check for the balance, and that the doors of Club 58 would be locked on New Year's Eve, unless I could get a check to him within the next couple of hours.

This was blindsiding. I immediately launched into an argument, insisting that JoonBug had delivered the check as per our agreement. "I can show you your signature on the receipt to prove it!" I sputtered.

But it was like talking to a wall. Stratis refused to even hear me out. And meanwhile, our office was in its usual pre-New-Year's pandemonium, with phones ringing off the hook and hundreds of people lining up to pick up the tickets they'd ordered. All big nights were like this, but New Year's Eve in particular was super crazy. We always had to start beefing up our staff from early November through January, just to help with all the calls, pickups, and other tasks.

It was my job to run around putting out fires and solving technical issues, and I just didn't have time to argue with Stratis over this bizarre miscommunication. To cut through the problem as quickly as possible, I looked online to see if the check I'd written on Tuesday had cleared or not, and it hadn't. So, I made out a second check and had my assistant jump into a cab right then to deliver it personally. Problem solved.

Only … with all of the chaos going on, it slipped my mind to call the bank and stop payment on the *first* check. I just moved on to the next emergency and didn't remember the check until much later.

Cash Crash

New Year's was on a Saturday that year, so, as it turned out, I wasn't able to call the bank until the following Monday. I picked up the phone and called bright and early, giving them the check number, and requesting a stop payment.

There were a few seconds of silence, as the teller worked on my request. And then she gave a courteous apology and said that the check had already been cashed.

My stomach dropped to my shoes. "I'm sorry, what?" I asked.

Her polite, businesslike voice repeated the awful truth: the check already had been cashed—and so had the second, identical check I had sent to Stratis the day before the party.

I couldn't believe what I was hearing. The next hour saw me rushing to the Commerce Bank branch on 26th and 7th, demanding to know how and why they had seen fit to cash both checks in one business day.

The manager came out to discuss the matter with me and protested. "He brought his ID and came directly to our branch, we checked your signature on the checks against the signature we keep on file, and there was enough money in the account to cover the checks…"

It was all so unbelievable. My blood pressure was rising with every second. "Why didn't you at least call me first? Didn't it seem at all suspicious to you that this guy was cashing two identical checks, for the exact same amount?"

This did not go over well. The manager basically kicked me out of the branch, huffily stating that he wouldn't speak to me any further until I "calmed down."

I found myself out on the sidewalk, flabbergasted. What to do next? The only option seemed to be reaching out to Stratis, but I had no faith that this would be successful. Still, I rushed back to the office and frantically called him on every phone number I had. As expected, he completely ghosted me. I couldn't get any kind of an answer, no matter how many messages I left with his staff. One of the managers of the club even lied to my face, saying, "Oh, Stratis isn't here—I actually haven't seen him in a long time!" I could practically hear him grinning. "Why don't you call again tomorrow?"

So, that was it. Stratis was hiding out, knowing full well that his scummy trick was tantamount to theft. But since it was a civil matter, the only legal recourse I had was through the civil courts—no matter how blatantly criminal his behavior had been!

Hell Hath No Fury

After several days of fruitlessly trying to get ahold of Stratis, I thought it would be best for Ariana to go to his office and try to talk to him in person. I thought it would be a lot harder for him to keep up the scam while looking her in the eye. Also, perhaps the fact that he had stolen from a young woman would shame him into giving the money back.

Ariana went to the club alone. As luck would have it, the moment she stepped inside the doors, Stratis appeared from a different door across the lobby. The two of them recognized one another immediately. Stratis stopped in his tracks, staring. Then, without a word, he bolted into his office and locked the door.

"Hey!" Ariana shouted, breaking into a run. The door shut and locked just before she reached it, and she pounded on its paneled surface, yelling, "I saw you! I know you're in there! You freaking scumbag *thief*!" But no matter what she said or did, he just kept silent, too chicken to confront her.

After a few minutes, one of the managers came up and told Ariana that she would have to leave, or they would call the police. To add insult to injury, he condescendingly added, "Nobody's in that office."

Another failure. It seemed there was nothing more to be done, so Ariana grudgingly came back to JoonBug's offices and told me what had happened.

Party Pooper

I was so furious I couldn't think clearly. My ego was getting the better of me. Just how hard we had worked on the event kept running through my mind. All that time, effort, and money, and for what? To end up in the negative by more than $150,000!

And there was more. Not only had Stratis cheated us with the checks, but he had also done an absolutely crappy job with the party itself. We'd gotten a ton of complaints after the party about all kinds of issues. The food we had planned was nowhere to be seen, the open bar had closed two hours earlier than it was supposed to, and the bartenders had been agonizingly slow in getting drinks out, except to the few guests willing to fork over outsized tips. The whole thing was completely different than advertised, and it was all Club 58's fault.

The poor quality of the event was so blatant that many of our ticket buyers actually called their credit card companies requesting chargebacks, which are basically refunds billed back to the merchant. That caused us a ton of headaches. Chargebacks ruin a business's reputation with the credit card company, so you end up paying more to keep working with them. On top of that, every chargeback cost us a $25 fee, regardless of whether or not we could successfully dispute it.

Thankfully, our disputes were usually successful, because we had a refund policy in place and disclaimers on every email, ticket, and event posting. But the hassle of formally disputing hundreds of chargebacks still cost us considerable time, money, and personnel. And for any unsuccessful dispute, we got slapped with additional fees, plus the chargeback fee, plus the price of the entire ticket order!

Call the Law

It was more than I could take. I picked up the phone and called my lawyer, directing him to initiate a lawsuit against Stratis and his company. My lawyer was against this idea, and rightly so. He told me what I already knew: a civil lawsuit against Stratis would be a long, drawn-out process that would almost certainly end up costing more in legal fees than I could possibly recover, even if we won.

But I didn't care, and neither did Ariana. We needed revenge! The only way we could feel better going forward was if we could somehow punish Stratis and his minions for cheating us and ruining our carefully crafted event. We went forward with the lawsuit.

Sadly, the whole thing went just as predicted. The legal bills mounted up, the suit dragged on, and in the end, Stratis and his partners abruptly shut down their company, declaring bankruptcy. That officially put a lid on our attempts to get back any of our money, much less the sweet revenge we had hoped for. All we got instead was a big, fat slice of humble pie, and a hard-learned but valuable lesson: When things go terribly wrong (and they will), don't live in the past, and don't seek revenge. Just move on to the next.

An Expensive, Priceless Lesson

That event not only cost us money, but it also cost me my peace of mind and time, two priceless assets that I could have been using on another project or event to make us money! I vowed not to let it happen again and turned my attention toward taking JoonBug to the next level, rather than making up for past injustices.

A Horrifying Halloween

I had just spent six months building a custom barcoded e-ticketing ticketing system that replaced old physical tickets with foil seals and ticket numbers that we had been using for our events. We also spent tens of thousands of dollars and countless hours buying and programming handheld barcode scanners to scan the new e-tickets. The system was finally ready, just in time for Halloween. We decided to launch it for one of our big events: Capitale. Since we usually sold thousands of tickets for that party, doing e-tickets would save us a significant amount of time and money, right out of the gate.

As hoped, the sales for the party went really well. We got far fewer calls about shipping, no calls at all about lost tickets, and had none of the hassle of stuffing envelopes, paying for shipping, or having customers lined up down the block, anxiously waiting to pick up in person. Things were going so perfectly that it almost seemed too good to be true … and it was!

No Charge

Part of working at JoonBug, even for "daytime" employees, was helping out with big events at night. Everyone did their part, jumping in as cashiers, ticket checkers, "runners" who helped patrol the event and look out for problems—essentially, whatever was needed.

Brooke and Liz, our assistants, usually took care of bringing all the supplies to our events. They'd load up bags with clipboards, pens, papers, cash boxes, VIP stamps, and all the rest and unload it all at the venue. This time, they added four barcode-scanning handsets!

Josh, our marketing guru, and John, one of our graphic designers, were slated to scan the tickets that first night. We all arrived at

Capitale early to set up, about an hour before the doors opened. And right away, we were hit with the first of what would become an avalanche of problems.

When I got to the doors, everyone was busily setting up all the necessities for admitting patrons. But Josh had taken one of our scanners out of the box and was standing there stock-still in the middle of all the activity, looking at it in puzzlement. "This isn't turning on," he said, frowning.

I felt a slight sinking in my stomach but tried to ignore it. Taking the scanner myself, I pressed the power button, but no matter how many times I pressed it or how long I held it down, nothing happened. It was dead as a doornail. Then it hit me: the scanners hadn't been charged! Somehow, we had forgotten to make sure we charged them up before coming to the venue.

To top it all off, we had forgotten to bring the chargers. They were still at our office in Chelsea. That sinking feeling was getting worse, but I told Josh to jump in a cab and go get them. It would probably take twenty minutes for him to get there and back, but that would leave forty minutes to charge up the scanners. It would be tight, but I figured that we could at least start scanning tickets with two, while the other two kept charging, and then switch when the first set lost power. At worst, we would just be switching handsets throughout the evening.

I was relieved when Josh got back in record time, and even more relieved when the scanners were successfully docked and turning on. Things seemed to be back on track, so I moved on to the final walk-through with Ariana and talks with staff and security.

Can't Win for Losing

When it was time to start, a line was forming outside the venue, and the scanners were halfway charged. That seemed like a great sign! Everyone was pumped as we opened the doors, and Josh scanned the first ticket.

Error. The scanner immediately threw a code, saying that the ticket couldn't be found. That was strange, but maybe there was just some issue with that particular ticket, so we asked the next person in line for her ticket.

Error. OK, not good. I was starting to sweat but tried not to read too much into it. If it wasn't the tickets, it must be the scanner. Luckily, we had more than one, right?

I tried the other scanner. *Error.*

I grabbed the other scanners from their charging docks and tried, but you guessed it: error codes all around. None of the tickets were scanning!

Meanwhile, the line was growing exponentially, and everyone in the crowd was getting agitated. My mind and heart were racing. Time was running out, but I couldn't formulate a next step.

Thankfully, Ariana jumped in. "I'll send Liz to the office. She can print out the ticket list, and we can check the numbers manually." It was the best option we could think of at the moment, and possibly the only option there was. Liz hurried away and we held the line, apologizing to the patrons and explaining that we were having technical difficulties. I was still trying everything I could to fix the scanners ten minutes later, when Liz called.

"I'm stuck, traffic is at a standstill!" she wailed. The nightmare was getting worse, and my anxiety was through the roof. I was so stressed that it was a struggle to think. Again, Ariana had an idea: she asked Liz what street was jammed, and then jumped in a cab herself to take an alternate route back to the office. At least one of us had a clear head!

By that point, it was almost twenty-five minutes past the time the doors should have opened. The crowd was super frustrated, yelling, and even demanding refunds. And unlike some other years, it was cold, which made people even more agitated. As things got more and more tense, Ariana called to say that she couldn't get the ticket list to print. I couldn't believe it. In that moment, it felt like the whole universe was conspiring against us.

After the Beep

Not one for giving up, Ariana started taking screenshots and printing them, one by one. But doing that took forever, and we were out of time. I walked outside and took a deep breath. From frantically racing this way and that, my perception seemed to suddenly shift; I saw everything in slow motion. My phone, ringing incessantly in my pocket. The line of angry patrons, shifting and frustrated. The looks of despair on our employees' faces. They'd never seen us sweat like that, and it was freaking them out.

I needed a solution. Suddenly, as if responding to my thoughts, a voice from the crowd rose above the rest. "Just let us in already!"

In a flash, I suddenly saw what to do, and it was so easy! I grabbed the scanners and pulled Josh and John to one side. "Listen—at this point, we have to let everyone in. It doesn't matter if their tickets are real or fake or get scanned or not. What we're going to do is just scan the tickets. I know it's going to give an error message, but that doesn't matter. Just scan the tickets and when the scanner beeps, let them in. Everyone with tickets gets in, and we'll deal with any issues as they come along."

The guys were totally on board, so we opened the ropes and started scanning tickets frantically. The crowd was relieved and actually cheered us, pouring into the club at a steady pace. The atmosphere changed, and so did everyone's mood. For my part, I was so relieved and happy that I forgot to call Ariana and tell her what was going on! A short time later, she came running up the steps of Capitale clutching a huge packet of printed papers, looking confused.

"Did you fix the scanners?" she called, puffing in the cold air as she ran toward me. Once she got closer, I pulled her aside and explained the situation in a whisper. Ariana's face went from concerned to happy, and she laughed at how simple the solution had turned out to be. Everything was now rolling along perfectly, and the party looked fantastic, which more than made up for the whole crazy fiasco.

Freedom!

But … it only took about twenty more minutes for something else to go wrong. We forgot about charging the scanners and suddenly we realized that they were all dying or dead. John and Josh looked at me with an "Uh oh, now what" expression. For a minute, I was stumped.

But the reality was, it didn't matter if we scanned tickets or not. We had decided to do that, so it seemed like that was our only option. But we could just as easily decide something else. Finally, I said, "OK, put the scanners away. From now on, take the tickets, and if they look legit, just take a pen and mark a big X on it so it can't be used again." That was it! Simple, effective, and liberating.

I was so amped up after that night that, once the event was over and I got home, I didn't go to sleep. Was it five in the morning? Yes. Did I care? No! I immediately got to work on a standard operating procedure and a backup plan for our new scanner tech. From that point on, we would always need to make sure the scanners were charged, that we brought the chargers, and that we had a laptop plus printout of the ticket information. All of this needed to be double-checked by two people prior to the event to make sure it was done correctly.

I also found out later that the scanners automatically wiped all data when they died, so that was another contingency we had to plan for. We ended up doing some mock testing, mimicking a real-life event, to make sure we could switch from one handset to another without losing battery life and data. Even after we implemented our plans, got new scanners, and mock-tested everything, there were still hiccups and mistakes. But having learned some lessons the hard way, we had contingency plans in place, and that made all the difference. The faster you accept the inevitability of problems and focus on being flexible, adapting, and staying one step ahead, the better off you'll be.

Nightlife Lessons Learned

Whatever can go wrong, *will* go wrong: it's Murphy's Law. Be comfortable with being uncomfortable. Most of the time you are the only person who is aware that something is amiss anyway. If everyone sees you panicking, they will start to panic, too! You have to remain calm and in charge whether the police show up, the fire department shows up, the DJ doesn't show up, or the electricity goes out. You never know what will happen. But be confident and you can figure things out, and it will all be OK. Don't forget the corollary to Murphy's Law: If there's a way to get screwed over, then you *will* get screwed over. You may have a contract in place, but that doesn't mean the terms will always be honored. There are so many times where we were supposed to get paid, and an intimidating bouncer would be sent by an owner and say: "It's not happening. Go home." Anywhere from $5,000 to $10,000 could be lost on a single event. In the course of a year, over $100,000 could be lost just by getting screwed over. That was simply the cost of doing business.

In retail they chalk that up as theft loss. Restaurants and grocery stores call it spoilage. It's going to happen. You will inevitably get screwed. The trick is to minimize it by learning from each getting-screwed experience, so you get a little less screwed the next time!

As if to prove how ubiquitous Murphy's Law is, something even more difficult and frightening happened with my next business: EZ Texting became the defendant in a class-action suit.

I'd never dealt with anything like that. A class action lawsuit is a very serious problem that can easily destroy a small business. Having to pay out damages could and probably would have led to bankruptcy and EZ Texting's shut down.

We were accused of violating the Telephone Consumer Protection Act, or TCPA. The allegation was that the plaintiffs were receiving text messages from our service that they hadn't consented to receive. EZ Texting began to suffer immediately because I was so preoccupied with the lawsuit. I had to learn the intricacies of complex law concepts and how to fight and survive.

I thought I had a good defense, since it could be argued that EZ Texting was just a service our customers were using to send out their own business SMS messages. But the class action plaintiff's lawyers knew how stressful and expensive defending ourselves would be, and they took full advantage. To end the pain and uncertainty, I ended up settling—but just a month later, we got sued again. Murphy's Law in action!

At this point, I knew I had to hire the best telecom lawyer in the country. The first thing he said to me is, "Shane, I know this isn't what you want to do. But the only way we can do this is to change or get a clarification of the law." I won't get into the details, but I suddenly became a lobbyist, petitioning the FCC and meeting with them in Washington. When Murphy's Law is the issue, adaptability and persistence are the answer.

I also realized that, since I was petitioning the FCC, I could ask that the judge in the new case stay the previous case until the FCC ruled on my petition —which might take up to ten years! That in itself became a deterrent and helped protect EZ Texting, because class action lawyers are looking for money now, not decades from now.

I powered against Murphy's Law and got through. Sometimes one smart move or decision can create an exit from a tough situation—if you're willing to fight hard enough for it.

NICHES FOR THE RICHES

DURING MY YEARS IN THE nightlife industry, I witnessed the same phenomenon over and over again: the riches in the niches. Certain party promoters avoided mainstream event promotions and instead went all-in on a particular niche, whether it was ethnic, demographic, religious, musical, or a particular holiday. These promoters were able to pull thousands of people to their events and made a fortune doing it. They found niche demographics that were large enough to be profitable and tailored their businesses to dominate that niche.

Under the Radar

Running JoonBug gave me the opportunity to meet every kind of promoter and club owner under the sun. Since we were the only game in town when it came to finding out about nightlife online, JoonBug was popular and well-known to the point of being ubiquitous. All kinds of promoters and organizers reached out to us, and I always found it especially interesting and inspiring to see how the different niche promoters operated. These guys were super-focused on one demographic and operated outside of the mainstream club scene.

The venues they used were sometimes dedicated entirely to the demographic they served: for example, gay bars or karaoke joints serving NYC's Korean community. Other times, they simply focused on packing out less-well-known (and more affordable) places, rather than competing to book the latest ultra-exclusive hotspot. It was a system that worked for them and the patrons they served, even though it was nothing like the flashy style of high-end promoters. Rather than turning up in the tabloids surrounded by models and celebs, these niche promoters made tons of money under the radar, and they liked it that way!

All-Inclusive Meets Niche-ing Down

JoonBug welcomed doing business with all kinds of promoters and club owners. The more events we handled, the more people visited our website, the more data we captured. JoonBug served as a hub, a place where you could find out about virtually any kind of event, from the hottest nightclub parties going on that week, to charity events that cost thousands of dollars per ticket, to an after-work happy-hour party or a Jewish singles speed-dating event. Any niche was welcome, regardless of race, ethnicity, creed, religion, or taste.

We did well with an all-inclusive approach because people usually occupy more than one niche. We knew that if we got data from someone because of a happy hour at a pool hall, for instance, those same people could be interested in salsa dancing, hip-hop music, other niche events, and, most importantly, our own large mainstream events.

While the JoonBug website was an aggregator of all different types of year-round niche events, our events arm also had its own niche: our two main events of the year, Halloween and New Year's Eve. On those nights, tons of people from all kinds of demographics came out to party. Despite all the events we promoted for other people, the events that we did ourselves accounted for around 50 percent of our total revenues annually, and half of that came from Halloween and New Year's Eve! It all came full circle; we got the customer database to promote these two mega-events from all those smaller niche events our site listed throughout the year.

Niches. That's where you find the riches. And with that in mind, allow me to reminisce about a few of the most lucrative and interesting niche promoters I met during my time in the industry.

Rapper's Delight

In the '90s, the hip-hop scene exploded and catering to its fans became a highly lucrative niche. Smart promoters recognized the trend, leaned in, and got rich.

Derek Corley

One niche promoter we worked with frequently was Derek Corley, who dominated events in the urban and hip-hop scene. He was well-known for doing the biggest, baddest high-end parties in that genre. His promotions company was called Black Diamonds, and the events he did became known as "Black Diamond Parties." They were incredibly popular because everyone knew that at a Black Diamond party, some big hip-hop or sports star would inevitably show up and cause a mob scene, or even better, give an impromptu performance. Derek packed out all the venues he promoted three or four nights a week. He was printing money just working with the demographic that loved hip-hop music and culture.

One interesting thing about Derek's parties was that everyone, without exception, paid a door charge to get in. The charge was something like $20 or $30 (which would be $40 or $60 now). Bottle service cost anywhere from ten to fifty grand. That would get you a table and bottles of whatever alcohol was the crème de la crème at the moment: Ace of Spades, Kristal, Dom Perignon, Nuvo, or Courvoisier.

Even celebrities paid because Derek didn't comp VIPs. Instead, he created an atmosphere in which buying a table and drinks for the whole club was seen as a status symbol. Conspicuous consumption and notoriety were what his swanky clientele wanted to display, and Derek gave them the ultimate platform for it, night after night.

Bill Spector

Derek wasn't the only hip-hop promoter in town. Another unlikely hero of that scene in the '90s was Bill Spector, a religious Jewish kid who had grown up on the Lower East Side.

Chubby, carefree, and whip-smart, Bill had a great sense of humor and a lot of charm. He could make anyone his friend in no time flat, thanks to his fun-loving personality. In the '80s, he was a big part of the nightclub scene, doing parties with Noel Ashman and DJ Mark Ronson (before Ronson became the Grammy-award-winning producer he is today). Bill often put on events at hot spots such as El Flamingo and China Club and became famous in the industry.

With the '90s, big changes were coming, and Bill knew he had to make changes as well to stay relevant. He transitioned to the hip-hop niche, incorporating hip-hop music, fashion, and celebrities into his already-impressive promotions game. It worked perfectly. Bill not only attracted a huge new following of hip-hop enthusiasts but also retained many of his other patrons, essentially building a new, eclectic, but mainly hip-hop-focused niche of his own. He aligned himself with celebs, musicians, and actors that were in the hip-hop niche and took it from there. People flocked to his events, lapping up the trendy new hip-hop aesthetic. The parties kept going, the cash kept flowing, and Bill kept crafting amazing experiences for the crowds that loved him.

Jessica Rosenblum

A lot of people may not realize that one of the major forces behind the explosion of hip-hop in NYC was actually a Jewish blonde bombshell named Jessica Rosenblum. She got her start in the world of nightlife working the door at Nell's, one of the most notorious clubs in all of NYC during its run—and one of the hardest to get into. It was owned by Nell Campbell, most famous for playing Columbia in *The Rocky Horror Picture Show*, and was decorated as a shabby, old-fashioned "club" in the sense of an English gentlemen's establishment.

Everyone from Andy Warhol to Eddie Murphy had frequented Nell's, and one of its attractions in the '90s was its unique musical experience, which some have called a laboratory of music. Funk, soul, and eventually hip-hop were popular there, with the likes of Puff Daddy and DJ Stretch Armstrong first making names for themselves in its small, Victorian surroundings.

Jessica met literally every celebrity, manager, and VIP as the doorperson of Nell's and became semi-famous herself because of that job. Using those connections, she was able to pivot and seamlessly transition into promotions as well as managing hip-hop DJs. To showcase the DJ Funkmaster Flex, she invented a now-legendary Sunday night hip-hop party, Mecca, which eventually found a long-term home at Tunnel hosting upward of 3,000 people each night, and in doing so Jessica became an almost legendary figure in establishing hip-hop culture in NYC. She was a powerhouse in the scene, and the stars she worked with included Russell Simmons, Funkmaster Flex, Busta Rhymes, and Puff Daddy, from the start of their careers into the present. As unlikely as it was to find a young, white woman running with the big dogs of hip-hop, and in some cases more or less managing their careers, Jessica did just that.

Network = Net Worth

Although elite promoters tended to scoff at bridge-and-tunnel crowds from NYC's outer boroughs—Long Island, Queens, Brooklyn, and the Bronx—masses of bridge-and-tunnel patrons poured into Manhattan week after week to party in "the city." It was a demographic too enormous for anyone to ignore, or at least for any smart person to ignore! So naturally, some promoters made it their (very profitable) business to cater specifically to those crowds.

Clique Promotions

A major player in the bridge-and-tunnel niche was Clique Promotions, a team of five guys whose combined talents birthed a mega-successful promotions company. Each one of them had grown up in NYC, and all of them loved to party. Young, hungry, good friends, and super smart, the five of them made bank catering to their huge joint network spread across the five boroughs.

All of Clique's members have gone on to do big things: Jase Kim became an executive at Pernod Ricard and is now at Lacoste. Nick Andreottola currently runs a big luxury concierge business. Johnny Dimatteo started a large electronic music concert promotions company, and Alex Cordova is a dynamo in the Las Vegas nightlife scene. Finally, there's Richie Romero, who now owns a number of clubs and restaurants in NYC and also became a partner at Butter Group.

Clique was one of the biggest players in the bridge-and-tunnel scene, especially popular among Italians from Staten Island and Howard Beach and Hispanics from Queens. Along with their large word-of-mouth grapevine, they employed a network of sub-promoters, and that was a key component of their success.

These sub-promoters weren't big-time. Each of them might only bring ten or twenty people to a given event. They worked for a cut of the door revenue, based on the number of people they rounded up, and Clique had systems in place to keep track of who invited whom.

That may sound like more trouble than it's worth. Why bother working with a bunch of small-time promoters who can only get ten people to your event, when you need hundreds or thousands of patrons in order to pay the bills and make a profit? Why bother with the hassle of tracking and paying percentages on little handfuls of patrons here and there?

For Clique, the answer was volume. If you have fifty sub-promoters, each bringing fifteen people on average to your party, that's 750 people right there. Plenty of venues would be considered packed out at that number!

Teaming Up, Moving Up

When we were doing our regular Saturday night party at Guastavino's, they asked us if we could put them in touch with someone who'd be a good fit for a Friday night event. We introduced them to a bunch of promoters we knew, including Bill Spector and the guys at Clique Promotions.

For our part, the incentive to help out was more than just networking for the sake of networking (although that can be useful). Even though we didn't directly make money from the Friday night party at Guastavino's (and, in fact, had our own Friday night party at Veruka to promote), a killer party on that evening would help put Guastavino's on the map. In turn, that extra notoriety would help our Saturday night party do even better!

And that was how it worked out. Within a few weeks, the Clique team and Bill were absolutely crushing it. They had a great mix of hip-hop crowds and bridge-and-tunnel crowds—who all paid to get in. The money was crazy, not only from charging at the door, but also from bar sales. And the buzz it generated got a lot of hip-hop stars there—and sometimes on our Saturday nights, too.

Mix It Up

Over time, the hip-hop/bridge-and-tunnel mix that flooded Guastavino's on Friday nights started to come to our more mainstream Saturday night party as well, and vice versa. That made Friday and Saturday nights at Guastavino's under the bridge a Mecca not only for the outer boroughs, but also for the brightest lights in hip-hop.

We were psyched beyond belief. Our parties might not have been the most exclusive, but they were increasingly popular and insanely profitable, and that was what mattered to us! We wanted all the niches, in order to get all the riches—especially the priceless riches of data.

Falling In Love

With Guastavino's being so close to our apartment, I would often end my Friday nights there, checking things out, meeting new people, and just keeping tabs. About a month into the Friday night party, I made one of my usual appearances, and it turned into a night I will never forget. It was about two in the morning, and Funkmaster Flex was spinning for an ecstatic crowd. Even at that hour, there was still a huge line outside the door, hoping to get in. Suddenly, the DJ scratched the record, and the music came to a halt.

The DJ booth was on an upstairs mezzanine, which also served as the VIP area, and I was standing up there alongside a makeshift bar for guests who were VIP enough to be on the mezzanine, but not VIP enough for a table. Flex's voice boomed out through the speakers.

"Yo, yo, yo!" he said. "I need quiet in the house—we have a special surprise for y'all!" It took about ten minutes before the patrons quieted down enough for Flex's taste. But eventually, in the relative silence, the sound of a piano could be heard. Guastavino's had a huge, gorgeous grand piano on the second floor, about ten feet from the bar where I stood. Usually, it was only for display. But Bill had apparently figured out the ultimate way to put it to use. I turned to see who was playing, and there was Alicia Keys, fluidly sounding out the opening bars of "Fallin.'"

Everyone in the VIP area was in shock, while others farther from the action struggled to understand what was going on. But when Alicia belted out the first line of the song, everyone got it, and after one second of electric silence, complete pandemonium broke out! In fact, Alicia Keys had to stop and start over, because they were drowning her out!

When the crowd and the singer finally synced up, the energy was incredible. Alicia delivered an amazing rendition of her first hit, even dancing on the piano bench without missing a beat.

And when she got to the chorus, everyone instinctively joined in, filling Guastavino's cavernous space with thousands of voices. It was truly magical.

The "Desi Party" Don't Stop

In New York City, there's a huge South Asian population, and Manny Singh was a promoter who served that demographic with incomparable know-how. He called his company Desi Party, "desi" being a colloquial term for someone of Indian, Pakistani, or Bangladeshi descent.

Manny's crowds were mostly first-generation South Asian immigrants and their children, who still had close cultural ties to their homelands. He knew everyone, and the numbers he did running weekly and monthly parties, Halloween events, Thanksgiving Eve events, and New Year's events rivaled the numbers we did at JoonBug—all without the use of cutting-edge technology or a massive database like we had.

Manny worked with JoonBug at times, hiring us to take photos of his events or list the events on our site and sell the tickets. So, we had inside information on how well he really did, and the methods he used. When I discovered just how profitable his business was, I was shocked.

In fact, I tried to figure out how JoonBug could implement some of his strategies and tactics. But what he was doing really couldn't be replicated digitally at that time. He had built a network of sub-promoters and employees within his target demographic who would put the network effects of today's Facebook and Instagram marketing to shame. It's one thing when an email or app tells you to go to a party. It's another thing when the most popular kids in your community tell you they're going to a party, and you should go, too. You can either join them or fall victim to the despair of incurable FOMO!

Another thing Manny had on lock was playing the right kind of music. His parties were usually Bollywood-themed and featured the most popular South Asian music played by one of a roster of DJs who were experts in that genre.

Interestingly, around that time, Bollywood culture also started to become popular in the world of hip-hop. From Dr. Dre (who was actually sued for sampling a hit song by an Indian artist) to Jay-Z to the Black Eyed Peas, hip-hop stars started incorporating Bollywood music, dance, and fashion influences into their own exploding scene. And when that happened, Manny started to do even better, because he wasn't just pulling in his South Asian demographic, he was also drawing in the growing and affluent hip-hop crowd!

There were many other cultural niches, based on people partying together and enjoying their shared heritage and traditions. For each of these niches, there were skillful promoters giving the people exactly what they wanted. There were specialized Korean promoters, usually in Koreatown; Chinese promoters catering to their demos; a Made in Italy Party that catered to "fresh off the boat" Italians and other Eurotrash; a Reggae scene frequented by Jamaicans and other Patwah speakers; and plenty more.

The Gay and Lesbian Scene

In my experience, the gay and lesbian scene was the most fun and outrageous of all. Those parties felt like the happiest and most friendly Halloween party, but on any night of the year. Lady Bunny, Amanda Lepore, Joey Arias, and many other celebrities in the scene were fixtures at these events, as well as at the more mainstream clubs. Each had their own style of dressing, speaking, and just being that made them famous.

One Queen to Rule Them All

But there was one personality in the scene who stood out above all the rest. Susanne Bartsch was (and is) an unrivaled master of NYC's queer nightlife, famous for her mega-parties and weekly parties that drew thousands from all over the tristate.

A Swiss who moved to London as a teen, Susanne brought British avant-garde fashion to an eponymous store in SoHo before she turned to fashion shows and then throwing nightclub parties. Being at one of Susanne Bartsch's parties was like an immersive theater experience, alive with sights, sounds, tastes, and more that you would never otherwise see or imagine in your wildest dreams. She made it big just focusing on the niche gay crowd, which also happened to draw in other niches because it was so over-the-top and fun. As a result, a huge segment of her niche ended up being not, in fact, LGBTQ+, but simply creatives there to experience the events she put on.

Susanne was so influential that even other promoters often went to her parties. This was a huge indicator of her prestige and capabilities, because normally, most promoters' egos were way too big for them to ever set foot in someone else's party!

Suffice it to say that she would, and still does, make a killing on all her parties. She plays the part well, sharing the drag queen aesthetic even though she's not one. In fact, The Museum at FIT even collaborated with her on a retrospective in 2015 called "Fashion Underground: The World of Susanne Bartsch."

One Big Matzo Ball

In 2006, Ariana and I decided to try throwing our own Matzo Ball Party. A Matzo Ball Party is held on Christmas Eve, and although of course many non-Christians and Christians go out on Christmas Eve, the event is geared mainly toward Jewish people who don't celebrate Christmas but still have the next day off of school and work. The name is a tongue-in-cheek nod to the Jewish focus of these kinds of parties, which are especially popular among Jewish singles looking to meet their future husband or wife.

With the large Jewish population in New York, we knew we would need a large venue for our Matzo Ball and decided there was no better choice than Capitale. After all, we were doing Halloween, Thanksgiving Eve, and New Year's Eve there every year. We might as well add one more to the list! So, we booked the venue, and a few weeks before the big day, we created all the artwork, photos, videos, and flyers for the event, posting them on our website. We called it "JoonBug's First Annual Matzo Ball Party."

Since it was our first-ever event like this, we also reached out to a few promoters who specialized in the niche. There were promoters who were popular in the Ashkenazi community, others who niched in the Syrian Jewish community, still others in the Persian Jewish community, the Sephardic community, and more—essentially, all the geographical sub-niches within the Jewish niche. We collaborated with all of them, giving them physical tickets to sell, as well as a special link for selling tickets online. The promoters earned a commission when purchasers used their dedicated link, making this one of the first online ticket sales affiliate programs ever.

Within the first week of advertising our Matzo Ball, we'd sold about 500 tickets. That was a good indication that we were going to sell a lot more. The vast majority of ticket sales happen in the two days prior to the event in question, so selling 500 tickets several weeks in advance was a very promising start.

I was super excited that we had found another massive event to add to our roster. My brain was on fire with plans for future Matzo Balls. We could book multiple venues for that night, not just in New York but in other cities as well. We could sell tens of thousands of tickets, just for one night out of the year!

But Murphy's Law had something to say about my plans. The next day, my dream bubble abruptly popped. A certified letter was delivered to our office, from a law firm representing, of all things, Matzoball™ Online. Yes. You read that right.

The letter basically said that by naming our event a Matzo Ball party, we were infringing on their trademark. They had trade-marked the term for their own party, which also fell on Christmas Eve and was called "Matzoball™." There was a copy of a lawsuit attached to the letter, and they stated that they were prepared to file it if we didn't cease and desist immediately. The letter closed with instructions to call a certain Andrew Rudnick if we wanted to discuss further.

At that time, I wasn't very legal-savvy, but I knew the letter was serious and could cause us a lot of trouble. I was horrified at the idea of getting sued, having to refund all those tickets, and losing all the money we'd sunk into the event. Worst of all, my grandiose vision of throwing massive and lucrative parties every year seemed dead.

The obvious thing to do was get our lawyer on the case, so that he could work things out with their lawyers. But I hesitated. Somehow, my gut was telling me that I could save everyone a lot of money and time if I just called this Andrew guy myself.

And in this rare case, that hunch turned out to be spot-on. When Andy first picked up the phone, he was hostile and surly. He started threatening me with lawsuits, trying to intimidate me by bragging about the fortune he was going to make off JoonBug because of the damages he'd suffered. Yada, yada, yada.

It was all a load of bull because he'd never even done a Matzo Ball party in NYC. Most of his parties at that time were in Miami, where he lived, and in Boston. I let him talk, and when he was done with his chest-beating, I calmly pointed out that "Matzo Ball" was a common term for the kind of party we were planning and explained that JoonBug had never heard of his company and trademark, and that we weren't trying to compete with him in any way.

That calmed him down a lot. Apparently, his threats and posturing were more or less part of a script that he used with tons of people every year, because there actually *were* companies out there using his trademark on purpose to peel off some of his customers. It turned out that he had to threaten them on a regular basis to remove the name from their events.

With that part of the problem cleared up, our conversation got a lot more cordial, and it wasn't long before we were having a normal chat about business. I was telling him about JoonBug and how we could even help him with promotions, using our digital tools.

It turned out that he did need some of the technology we had, including our ticketing system, email blasts, and of course our database containing lead info for people all over the country, not just New York City. Heck, we even discovered that we had some mutual friends! By the end of the call, we had formed a partnership. JoonBug would share some of our technology for a reduced fee and would give him a royalty cut for tickets we sold using the name Matzo Ball. In return, Andy would allow JoonBug exclusive rights to use the name for our events in New York.

It was a big win for everyone. We ended up selling thousands of tickets online as well as at the door, and our First Annual Matzo Ball was a huge success. In subsequent years, the Matzo Balls became some of the most profitable, popular, and fun events we did, rivaling even Halloween and New Year's Eve.

Nightlife Lessons Learned

It's rare to have a business that appeals to the masses, spanning dozens of demographics. And if you do go for that, chances are you'll face pretty steep competition out of the gate.

JoonBug did manage to excel at appealing to the masses, and that propelled us to great success. But along the way, I saw other people in the industry taking the niche approach and achieving fantastic success that way, year after year and decade after decade. One of my major takeaways from spending years in nightlife and hospitality is this simple but profound observation: for most entrepreneurs, focusing on a key demographic is the path to wealth.

But concentration on a niche only works well if you first evaluate the niche. Is it large enough to be profitable in the long run? Do you know enough (or can you learn enough) to cater to that niche effectively? And finally, the never-ending question: what can you do not only to serve but to *dominate* that niche? Concentration and domination are the keys to mining the riches in the niches.

However, don't try to create a niche— focus on one that already exists. There are Urban, Asian, Indian, Korean, Latin, and Jewish promoters that just focus on their own demographic and pull in thousands of people. They make a ton of money because they are still making a product that the masses want and serving their niche. In business, you make a lot of money by providing a specific service to a certain customer. There's no need to divert or expand into something else if what you are doing is working really well. Find a niche, stick to it, and make a ton of money.

At EZ Texting, we took a slightly different approach to "nichification" that ultimately paid off. When we were starting out in 2005, texting wasn't being used much for business purposes, especially in the U.S. We knew we had a valuable service, but one for which we'd need to create more demand and make texting seem like a mainstream business activity. Initially, we had no competition, so when someone searched the web with a term like "mass texting," the only result was EZ Texting.

It may have been a bit of a sneaky move, but we created a number of business texting "competitors" that were really just white-label versions of our software—the same software marketed under different names and through different websites. Anyone searching for "business texting" or similar terms would get numerous results, indicating that this was an in-demand service and growing industry—all of which made it more likely that they would want to learn more. This also had a side effect of deterring new competitors from coming into the space because they thought the competition was already fierce.

Each of these white-label "competitors" differentiated itself by addressing a different niche. We made websites just for nightlife, just for restaurants, just for churches, and for just about every vertical we could think of. That "company's" website content was dedicated to how you use texting for that niche, even though the underlying software that they were all funneled into using was exactly the same—just branded and skinned differently.

This caused EZ Texting revenue to really explode. Say, for instance, you're a restaurant owner and come upon "RestaurantTexting.com," and everything on the website is about how texting can help you promote your restaurant. Even though the underlying software is the same as that behind "ChurchTexting.com," you're persuaded into feeling that RestaurantTexting.com is exactly what you need.

In the venture capital space, my niche is focusing on founders who would appreciate working with previous founders. As a three-time business founder myself, I can connect on an emotional and psychological level with a lot of the founders I'm considering funding, and that gives me an edge over other VCs who are just writing checks and have never been down in the weeds building their own startups. Founders can talk to me about both the professional and personal struggles they're having, because I've been through them as well. I can also give them pragmatic advice that others can't.

THE PARTY ALWAYS COMES TO AN END

I GOT OUT OF THE nightlife scene when it got too taxing on my life. Running JoonBug essentially meant working all through the night until the early morning hours, crashing briefly, and then coming into the office a few hours later, blinking in the daylight and downing coffee like water. After nearly a decade in the industry, the constant hustle and long hours became unbearable, and it was time to move on. And it was time for Ariana and me to move on from each other as well.

Where Are They Now?

Of course, I wasn't the only one. Many of my friends and acquaintances from my days at JoonBug pivoted to new ventures, especially when marriage and kids became part of the equation. But getting out of the scene isn't for everyone; I know plenty of people who are still in the game twenty and thirty years later. If you can believe it, there are some old-school promoters who still love what they do at fifty years old, and older: going out, partying, and recruiting crowds.

Rocco Ancarola

I imagine Rocco is probably in his sixties by now, making him one of the oldest guys I know in nightlife. I first met him during my high school years, when he owned and ran the hotspot Boom in Soho, where people would come for dinner and routinely end up dancing on the tables and breaking cups and plates all night long. It was that kind of place! Rocco ran a party there on Sunday nights called Riviera Sundays, where the staff and entertainment would dress up in different themes. After Boom, he made a huge splash with his partnership in The Pink Elephant, which became one of the best-known clubs in the city—and he took Riviera Sundays with him.

Rocco is a former actor from South Africa with an unsurpassed charm and wit. He had (and apparently still has) a great knack for getting people to party their hardest and dance the night away. He's still in the nightlife business, and as far as I can tell, still going strong and married to the party, despite a heart attack several years back that put him out of the game for a year or so.

Riviera Sundays has literally been going on for decades, although it's now at Lavo for Sunday brunch in NYC. It's a big production— much more than it was back in the '90s—because Lavo is owned by Tao Group, and they have the money and unrivaled hospitality power to do much bigger and nicer things. Rocco still goes all out every Sunday with a different theme, putting on a whole production of drinks, food, and entertainment (primarily featuring scantily clad dancers, live music, and himself sporting a painted-on mustache) to get everyone dancing on the tables and having fun.

Scott Sartiano

Scott was 50 percent of the force behind Butter Group, which owns the 1OAK brand. He's arguably one of the best-known, A-list, celebrity promoters and owners ever. But a few years back, he got married, and he and his wife welcomed a baby, which most likely led to the realization that the nature of nightlife just doesn't jive with family life. After all, you can't stay out until six a.m. hosting parties and hobnobbing with celebrities when you have a wife and newborn at home who likely need your help—especially during those early morning hours!

In any case, Scott left his partnership with Richie and Butter Group and pivoted to a new enterprise. He started The Broken Coconut, a healthy fast-food chain in NYC, which allowed him to continue utilizing his skill set and contacts in the hospitality space while getting out of the more onerous aspects of club-oriented work. He also created Zero Bond, a swanky members-only club along the lines of London's Soho House.

Jayma Cardoso

Jayma was one of the most well-known people in the NYC nightlife industry for a time, mostly doing the door and running VIP host services at the hottest hardest-to-get-into spots in the city: first at

Pangaea and then at Cain. But after a good long run at those places, she basically left the scene. She does some private parties, and she opened the Surf Lodge in Montauk, a hotel, restaurant, and live music venue that focuses on things like yoga, wellness surfing, and live music and art. The Surf Lodge is probably the most popular place to go in that area and always super-crowded. It's basically impossible to book a reservation there, either for a room or for the restaurant. Jayma also started a family, which undoubtedly influenced her in that direction. I would be surprised if she's set foot in a nightclub in years!

Jon B

Although Jon B pursued a very nontraditional career, becoming one of the biggest promoters in New York City, over the years he became very traditional in his personal life. He had always kept kosher, but as he got older, he grew more religiously observant, including keeping the Sabbath. Eventually, he married a Persian girl with similar traditional values, settled down, and started a family. So, things came full circle: not only was he successful in business but in his personal life as well, building a loving family and a home.

He then became a famous restaurateur opening some hotspots in NYC, including Beautique, which won the Concierge Choice Award for Best New Restaurant in 2014, but had to pivot his hustle when COVID came along. Like many others and I, he ended up moving down to Miami, abandoning New York City for good.

The Great Real Estate Agent Migration

A significant number of former promoters, who either reached the age of retirement or had become exhausted by the lifestyle, turned to real estate.

It's almost impossible to keep up with bringing crowds of patrons to clubs year in and year out. Some people manage to do it, of course. But most promoters, as they age, don't want to keep living that life—and neither do their friends! If they try to keep going, they have to start going after younger and younger crowds, which means becoming the creepy old guy who keeps trying to hang out with the cool kids. There is definitely a shelf life for almost all promoters, at least in the business model they start out with.

COVID definitely hastened the trend of promoter-turned-real-estate-agent, but it was already a notable development. It also seems like a natural fit. Promoters can leverage their networks, selling, renting, and buying homes instead of tables—which are really just another form of real estate, when you think about it. They can use the same charm, wit, and wining-and-dining skills to convince people to work with them. Also, it's low risk and high reward since they make a base salary plus commission. And the test to get your license is, by some accounts, not much harder than a fifth-grade math test.

Two particularly notable promoters who chose the real estate path were Gordon von Broock and his brother Erik. These two were nightlife promoter royalty in years past, working at places such as Pangaea and Cheetah. Afterward, they went on to open and own multiple venues, including Chateau in the West Village and Tavern in Southampton. Now they're highly successful in the real estate industry.

Other promoters who turned to real estate included: Joe Messina, who did a lot of business with us at JoonBug when he was doing promotions; Redd Stylez, who worked for clubs such as Cain, Guest House, and more; Bernie Marshall, who transitioned from models and parties to luxury home sales and rentals in Manhattan; Scott Hockens, a broker in New York and Miami; and Chris Massey, who also does real estate in NYC.

The JoonBug Gets Squashed

By 2008, I realized that I truly needed to make some big life changes. JoonBug was seven years old, and a whole slew of events were converging in real time that made it clearer than ever that the party was ending, and I needed to get out.

Old and Tired

For one thing, I was getting older. I was thirty years old and literally could not remember sleeping through a whole night in the past seven years. The typical grind for me was going to the office around nine in the morning and working nonstop until about seven that night—or as late as eleven o'clock in October, November, and December, which were our biggest months. After my office work, I would go home to change and rest for a couple of hours, and then order in some food or hit a restaurant. Then it was time to go out, babysitting whatever event needed my attention until three or four in the morning. Finally, I could go home and sleep, but only for a short time, because I would soon have to be right back at the office.

I never did drugs, and I was careful not to drink too much, which I think is why I was able to survive living that way for so long. But after seven years, I was definitely tired out, both physically and mentally. Adding to my workload was my newfound business, EZ Texting; managing it as well as my work for JoonBug was beginning to be too much, and I started coming to work later and later. I no longer looked forward to the challenges and successes of JoonBug, but rather found myself dreading the investment of time and energy in a business I no longer enjoyed. There were days I wouldn't even come into the office, even though it was only a block away. Before that, I had practically lived in the office, sleeping on my couch there and working late into the night.

In contrast, EZ Texting was my shiny new baby. It showed so much promise and interested me so much that I struggled to focus on the routine of running JoonBug. In fact, I was starting to hate nightlife in general: the fakeness, the grind, the garbage, and the petty, shallow people involved in all aspects of it.

I desperately needed a new routine and a consistent sleep pattern. At this point, I was gaining weight from the sheer stress of my responsibilities and schedules—lack of sleep, lack of exercise, over-eating, and even sometimes getting drunk (something I had never done in the past) were all having a terrible effect on my well-being.

EZ Texting > JoonBug

At the same time, it was becoming clear to me that not only was I getting worn out—JoonBug itself had peaked, and it would all be downhill from there. The biggest problem was that, in order to stay relevant in the ever-evolving world of events, we had to reinvent the business every year. New venues, new owners, and the changing tastes of the crowds dictated our work, which meant that we had to continually reinvent ourselves in order to stay relevant. In turn, that meant keeping abreast of the latest trends in music, style, venues, gossip, celebrity culture, and all the rest—whether we wanted to or not.

Also, unlike a recurring-revenue business, in nightlife, you face a constant vicious cycle of renegotiating every business deal, every year. It was exhausting having to start over each time, securing the venues, selling the tickets, and taking on all the work and risk involved in running the events. If you can imagine it, we felt like we were having to rebuild our house every year, fighting and competing for every resource that we needed to build it, including the land that we had already leased many times over!

To make things even more stressful, right at that time three new technologies began to skyrocket to popularity: social media, cellphone cameras, and email/website software. Their success chipped away at ours gradually but steadily, making JoonBug more obsolete with every passing week.

The Rise of Social Media

Social media networks such as MySpace and Facebook were slowly but surely edging out JoonBug with respect to our super valuable database. By using social media, promoters and venues were able to get direct access to an arguably much larger set of people than JoonBug could muster. And social media came equipped with handy tools that allowed them to create their own promotions: scheduling events, posting flyers, and sending direct messages.

The network effect of friends sharing events and profiles that they liked was simply unbeatable. A savvy promoter could use social media to build up a huge network within months for very little money. It took time, sure, but in terms of dollars and cents, it was way cheaper than JoonBug!

The same was true with venues. They could just hire interns to build their network and send out online invites to everyone. We had some of that network effect and virality going on at JoonBug with our photos, but that would soon be severely compromised as well.

Along Came iPhones

The iPhone didn't just kill the BlackBerry; it killed our photo business. Once people had flash cameras with several megapixels, plus the ability to send and share photos easily, our entire photo business dropped dead. Fewer and fewer patrons cared about having their photos taken because they were already taking their own!

On top of that, venues and promoters increasingly found it cheaper to hire their own photographers to go around capturing their events. Not only did they stop paying us to send over our photographers, but they wouldn't even let our photographers in if we sent them over for free! We went from taking photos of ten to thirty events every night, with many more on weekends, to covering between one and five. And those were the same tired clubs, week after week.

Our SEO game was still crazy strong, and our database was still building because of that, but the rate of growth was diminishing rapidly. And the sales of printed photos? Those slowed down to a crawl of just a few orders each day. Nobody wanted to be bitten by the JoonBug anymore!

Email and Websites, Easy and Cheap

A third complicating development came in the form of user-friendly, effective software for sending out email campaigns and building good-looking websites. Companies such as Constant Contact were becoming very well-known through TV and radio ads, and they were super cheap to set up—in many cases, free. You could create a list of contacts and send professional-looking email newsletters and even gauge the effectiveness of your efforts by using their analytics suite. This was the same kind of data that the big boys used, now available to everyone!

Of course, every promoter, owner, brand, and their mother were sending out junk emails left and right. To make matters worse, big email companies like Hotmail and Gmail started lumping JoonBug into that same category. Not only were we just one of a ton of emails going out to advertise events, but we were also struggling like crazy to stay in everyone's inbox!

Similarly, DIY website builders and companies like GoDaddy made creating business websites and uploading photos a cinch. The whole incentive for promoters and venues to let us take care of their email and web advertising was gone. It was now easy and cheap to do it themselves. Most importantly, they started realizing the value of having their own data.

Change of Pace

From a business perspective, it was clear to me that EZ Texting was a far superior business to JoonBug. EZ Texting was growing exponentially, while JoonBug was lagging. EZ Texting had recurring revenue and required a lot less overhead and manpower to run, while JoonBug required endless days and nights of hard work.

Plus, a company like EZ Texting could sell for ten to fifteen multiples of revenue, whereas something like JoonBug would only sell for one or two multiples of revenue, max. Most people wouldn't even be interested in buying JoonBug, because even though we'd branded it to be easily transferable, the backend of the business dealing with owners and promoters was highly dependent on Ariana and me. She and I were the ones who had key relationships in place with venue owners, advertisers, promoters, and sponsors, and there was no guarantee that those relationships would transfer to the buyer.

My attention was so consumed by EZ Texting that it was having an effect on everything related to JoonBug, especially on Ariana, who was taking up a lot of my slack. We had stopped innovating on the technology side of things, and we weren't being aggressive with finding and securing new or overlooked venues anymore. Essentially, we stopped growing. From 2007 to 2008, we stagnated: it was the first year that we made the same amount of money as the year before.

Meanwhile, EZ Texting had new users signing up by the minute, with revenues growing exponentially by hundreds of percent every month. That freshness and growth made working on EZ Texting a lot more emotionally satisfying for me, which Ariana understood; she supported my efforts, but continued to make JoonBug her priority while I made EZ Texting mine. For me, JoonBug was becoming the ignored older sibling, outshone by the newborn—I still had a lot of love for it, but my new baby needed a lot of attention, which I willingly gave.

Ariana and Not Me

In terms of hard work, our schedule, and our feelings about drugs (none) and alcohol (not much), Ariana and I were really similar, which probably contributed to our relationship lasting as long as it did under the pressure of running JoonBug. But by 2006, the constant, 24/7 routine of working together, living together, eating together, and all the rest had taken a toll on our relationship. Slowly but surely, it came to an end.

My advice to anyone who is thinking of working with their significant other is this: you can try, but it's probably the quickest way to kill all the passion in your relationship. Everything eventually becomes about work, and no matter how you try to separate your personal life from your professional life, problems and disagreements will bleed over from one to the other. Before long, every aspect of your life, and the majority of your conversations, will be permeated with the pressures of running a business.

We were like those couples whose entire life ends up revolving around their child, eclipsing their relationship with each other. But because our child was our business, there was no one who could "babysit" for us—not even for one night. We were literally working all the time, in the office, out of the office, and each night as we headed out to monitor our events. The grind was relentless, and slowly wore away any hint of romance, until we had transformed from boyfriend and girlfriend into business partners who hung out with each other all the time and were also roommates.

Eventually, we broke up, and the breakup was as unconventional as our relationship had been. We still had to see each other all day and almost every night because of JoonBug. We were mature enough to know that JoonBug was bigger than both of us, and neither of us wanted to lose it—JoonBug was too successful and lucrative for us to let it fall apart. So, we put our personal differences aside and continued to work together but separated our personal lives completely.

Nevertheless, it was super difficult not to fight about personal stuff at work, and even more difficult to see one another going out on dates. You might think it would be easy to avoid that in a city the size of New York, but not for us. We both gravitated toward the same restaurants and hotspots, usually because we had friends there who made it easy and fun to show up.

Sometime later, both Ariana and I were in separate long-term relationships, but it was obvious that we would still struggle in our dating lives as long as we continued to work together. No one, guy or girl, wants their significant other spending every single day working alongside their ex! And I didn't need that kind of issue cropping up all the time. It was hard enough to find someone who didn't judge me from the get-go for being in the nightlife business.

Nightlife doesn't have the greatest reputation, at least for guys. I'm not sure how it was for Ariana. I think she probably had an easier time because guys would have been more likely to find her job intriguing and fun. But most girls wouldn't take me seriously, assuming that I was a player, all about partying and having a good time. What was ironic was that I was the exact opposite: always in long-term relationships, looking for someone to settle down with and possibly marry.

By late 2007, Ariana and I knew it was time for another change. The business continued to be exhausting, and we weren't getting any younger. Each of us wanted to find the right person, get married, and start a family, but the lifestyle that JoonBug required us to live was not conducive to any of that. We didn't want to wait until we were much older: the older you get, the harder it is to find someone to settle down and possibly have children with. If we wanted real relationships, we had to somehow leave JoonBug behind. The only question was, how could we do that in a way that made economic and logistical sense?

Saying Goodbye

As 2007 drew to a close, we found ourselves starting all over once again. It was our busiest time, and we had to figure out our lineup, negotiate and renegotiate contracts with venues, fire up our promotions, make an ad budget, and juggle all the other details that come with the holiday season. As I've explained, it was becoming harder and harder to do all of this and turn a profit, because the price of basically everything had been driven up by competition. Other promoters were going after the same venues, the price of Google AdWords clicks rose dramatically, and everyone was sending out emails and social media blasts to the same crowd of people who liked to go out in NYC.

We had one competitor in particular, Jon Gabel, who ran Sky Events and Crave Tickets. He was constantly nipping at our heels, trying to get the same venues that we worked with. He even created a ticketing system similar to ours, with the difference being that he white-labeled his system to allow promoters and affiliates to brand the system as their own and sell tickets on their own websites.

Jon shared the customers' data with the promoters and venues and also took a fee for their use of his platform, usually in the form of convenience fees to ticket buyers. He also allowed promoters to sell tickets for his events on their own websites, giving them a cut of the proceeds. In a word, he brought sub-promoting to the digital age! JoonBug didn't do any of that stuff—we sold tickets to our own events and some others, period, and kept the data for ourselves. It was much more profitable and easier to manage that way, but it did cause a lot of resentment within the industry.

We were professional enemies at the time, so to speak. Nevertheless, after discussing it with Ariana, I picked up the phone one day and called him. I told him that, if he was interested and had the money, we could figure out some kind of a deal for him to buy JoonBug. He pounced, not wasting a minute, not asking any questions about why we were selling, nothing. That same afternoon, he was at our office, and we were banging out the details of a takeover deal.

Jon jumped at the chance to own JoonBug, knowing he was getting the best database and brand in the space. And not only that—he was also automatically inheriting our contracts that year for the best and biggest venues on New Year's and Halloween: Capitale, Guastavino's, Marquee, and Cain, among others.

Within a few weeks, the three of us settled on a price and terms that made sense for everyone involved. It was all very quick and friendly because both sides were motivated to get a deal done. Ariana and I wanted out, and we were willing to be flexible on the price in exchange for a fast transaction that would include having Jon take over Halloween and New Year's—while we still got paid! And Jon was very accommodating; he knew it might be his only chance at acquiring his biggest competitor, the one he'd been trying to catch up to for years.

Before long, the three of us were seated at a long meeting table in a fancy New York lawyer's office, preparing the paperwork for the sale. It was a whirlwind and blur that made my head spin a little. I remember feeling very conflicted about selling everything we had worked so hard to build, as well as overwhelmed by the wave of relief that washed over me. No longer would I have to go out every single night or deal with promoters and nightclub owners. I was getting out from under the stigma attached to the nightlife industry. Best of all, I would no longer feel conflicted about what I did with my time. I could focus fully on what I had come to love most: EZ Texting.

It was crazy to think that JoonBug—which had been the source of all my drive, meaning, purpose, and wealth, for so long—had become a burden I was willing to part with so easily. And not only that, but I was also parting with it for a sum of money which, although large at that time, didn't even come close to reflecting the pain, sweat, tears, adrenaline, and sleepless nights that had gone into the making of it.

It was all very strange. Once the transaction was done, all we would need to do was tell our employees and then simply walk away. There was no need for training, or introducing Jon's people to our clients, or anything else that is normally done when a company has been bought out. Jon already knew all the owners and promoters who usually contracted with us as clients, and he already had experience running a website, photo, and ticketing system. He had a whole tech team ready to take over.

For my part, I would be happy to take some of our JoonBug employees with me to work at EZ Texting, and I would use most of the proceeds from the sale to grow the EZ Texting business, secure new office space, and buy out Ariana's shares. It didn't make sense for us to sell JoonBug only to continue working together in a new venture. Ariana wasn't interested in working at a software company anyway. She loved events and would find something new to do in that field.

The final paperwork signing took place in our meeting room in the JoonBug/EZ Texting offices, which were one and the same. Before that happened, none of our employees knew a thing. And so, after the paperwork was signed, Jon, Ariana, and I stepped out into the main loft office space and gathered everyone together. We announced the sale right then and there. We told the employees who would be coming with me to EZ Texting, and we reassured everyone who was staying with JoonBug that their employment was safe and that Jon would take care of them. I began to pack up my few personal things, including my computer, some clothes, and my papers and files. It took maybe four or five hours to pack up what had taken years of my life to build. We said goodbye to those that were staying at JoonBug, and Ariana and I walked downstairs with everyone who would be coming with us to EZ Texting, giving Jon a few hours with the remaining JoonBug employees before going back upstairs to get our things.

The office had been strewn with thousands and thousands of printed photos over the years, collaged across the walls in a splash of color: thousands of partygoers and celebrities, and some of us, smiling and posing for the camera. But when I shut the door, the party ended for us. It had gone on too long for me anyway, personally and professionally; I felt like the last guest at a venue, overstaying my welcome. We left without looking back at those thousands of mostly anonymous people all over our walls. It wouldn't matter, anyway, to any of them; Ariana and I were just as unknown to them as they were to us since all they knew of us was the JoonBug logo.

Jon was taking over our lease and wanted to keep all the furniture and fixtures and space for his newly expanded team. So, we left things as they were, just removing ourselves and our belongings from the equation. It was uneventful, no fanfare or dramatic fare-wells. We shut off the lights, closed the door, and never came back. Ariana and I just stood there on the sidewalk looking at each other. I think we both felt a sense of disbelief that it was really over.

But we had taken things as far as we could in terms of both our business and our relationship. From that time on, we would seldom talk or see each other, and we were OK with that, truly happier for each other (and for ourselves) than sentimental or sad. We hugged each other and walked our separate ways, starting new journeys that we were each excited and ready to begin.

I knew I could handle the new challenges that awaited me, armed with the precious and crazy lessons I had learned. In New York, they say, "If you can make it here, you can make it anywhere." What's even more true is that if you can make it in New York City nightlife, you can make it anywhere, anytime, and under any conditions. In an industry notorious for chewing people up and spitting them out in a matter of months, I had survived—and thrived—for nearly a decade. And our legacy would live on through another owner who would keep JoonBug alive and buzzing.

For a few months after that, I took a hiatus from going out in NYC. When I did go out to a nightclub again, it was different. This time, I was at the party as a civilian, and I genuinely had fun. I could let go, enjoy the experience, and not worry about any of the details. Old friends and customers were working the door, hosting, and running around putting out fires that no other patron would have noticed except for me. I breathed a sigh of gratitude that I was on the other side of things, and for the first time in over ten years, went home at the end of the night and fell soundly asleep. No more replaying how the night had gone, and no more worrying about the next night's party!

Nightlife Lessons Learned

Selling JoonBug was a difficult decision because I exited while it was still successful. I didn't need to sell it, but I was also thinking about what the inherent risks would be if I didn't sell and all the things I would not be able to do otherwise. I left the party while it was still hot. Perhaps the party would rage on for a long time afterward, but I didn't know that for sure. And there were other kinds of parties I wanted to have.

All in all, I think it's very important to know when the party's about to end. Before things go on too long, look around and make plans to move on. Better yet, know this: the party might be over for you, but it might be a good time for someone else's party to start! So don't feel bad about leaving yours. Come to theirs and have a good time. And definitely have a sustainable plan in place for your own after-party.

The same situation basically happened much later with EZ Texting when I decided to sell the company. Eight years after founding it, I said to myself: "This party is really good. It's really awesome. I'm having the best time ever. Is it time to stop because maybe there are better parties out there that I'll enjoy just as much that won't take everything out of me? I can experience other things." Even though EZ Texting has grown tremendously since I sold it and is doing phenomenally well right now, I know I made the right decision for myself.

I wanted to have a family and to spend time with my children. Those things are very hard to do when you're running a very big business. There are people who do it successfully, but that doesn't mean it's not difficult. Again, I made a conscious choice to do what I felt was best at that moment in time.

For many people, when it comes to their business, they spend so much time, money, and energy on it that they conflate themselves with it. I've been lucky to be able to detach my identity from whatever my business has been.

Even though I had poured all my blood, sweat, and tears into both JoonBug and EZ Texting, I was willing to eventually let them go. This came naturally to me, but it's something anyone can learn. Some people get their sense of importance as well as identity from their business. To some degree you need that because you have to care enough about it to stick by it for long enough for it to become successful. You can't be completely apathetic toward it. But you also can't be so attached to it that it's literally one and the same as you.

Today, many venture capitalists are looking for founders who can't separate themselves from the business and are willing to spend all their waking hours hustling and growing their business. This is obviously not healthy for any founder and leads to early burnout. The point of existing is ultimately to be happy and to enjoy life. I don't think you can do that if you're completely identifying yourself only with your business.

Now, when I am wearing my VC hat, I look for a founder who's failed once or twice. The usual perception of failed founders is that they aren't committed or savvy. Counterintuitively, I think, if a founder gets back up after failing multiple times, then their odds of success are higher this time around. In their journey, they have probably learned a lot and likely won't make the same mistakes.

Success in business is a probability dance. You can do everything perfectly right and still have a bad outcome, and conversely you can do everything wrong and have a good outcome that only time will reveal. It's surely more of an art than a science. You're never going to be a hundred percent right. And that's perfectly fine as long as you can remember to be happy with that.

AFTERWORD

AS TECHNOLOGY EVOLVED AND BECAME more accessible, it slowly chipped away at the JoonBug business model, making it mostly obsolete in only a decade. Recently, COVID hastened even more changes that were on the horizon, proving that the internet could be used to replace in-person events. The future of the nightlife and hospitality industry is likely to be brought about by Web3 blockchain technology and located in the metaverse.

In the years after I sold JoonBug, email service providers such as MailChimp and Constant Contact enabled venue owners and promoters to build their own email lists and send out professional-looking emails en masse, while tools such as Wix, SquareSpace, and WordPress made it simple for them to create their own slick web presence. Companies such as EventBrite brought about quick and easy self-service electronic ticketing that could be used for any kind of event.

Meanwhile, high-resolution cell phone cameras eliminated the need for photographers at events. Instead, partygoers were taking their own selfies and posting them on social media, often in real time. That resulted in free advertising to the venue owners and promoters—who, in another new trend, were occasionally one and the same. Social media, including Facebook, MySpace, and Instagram, also allows promoters to take advantage of the network effects of these platforms through accessing friends of their friends. By widening their network, they are able to promote events to an ever-growing following.

The nightlife industry was becoming more sophisticated by 2013, especially at clubs such as Marquee that were owned by promoters. They would employ CRM solutions such as Salesforce and HubSpot to track and store information about their customers. That would typically include everything from a person's age and birthday captured from an ID scan, to food and drink orders, to what a head host or bottle waitress might record about how someone was dressed or who they came to the club with. This allowed promoters and venues to know exactly who their customer was and tailor attention accordingly, perhaps inviting a customer for a free bottle of their favorite kind of alcohol or sending a present on their birthday.

More recently, the state of nightlife and hospitality has gone down the road of exclusive membership clubs. These include places such as Soho House, Zero Bond, Casa Cipriani, and ZZ's in Miami. These clubs require you to apply for membership, obtain referrals from several other members, and pay an annual fee (much like an exclusive country club). Memberships usually come with access to the club's app where you can make reservations, see event schedules, connect with members, and access other choice benefits. Most importantly, membership comes with the prestige of being able to take your friends to a place where they would never be able to get in without you. You also hobnob with fellow members, all of whom went through the same selective application process and wallet drain to get in.

The advent of Web3 blockchain technology has already led to the development of an alternative to paper or e-tickets: NFT tickets. In this case, the NFT (non-fungible token) is a digital ticket that you buy with your credit card or cryptocurrency through an app. Your ownership is recorded in a public ledger (the blockchain), along with the ticket's ownership history (the chain of custody) and how much it was sold for each time.

Companies such as Yellow Heart and Tixologi already have technology for NFT ticketing, and each of their tickets bundles access to the event with additional perks, such as exclusive content, connection to other fans, loyalty points, and engagement with the artists. It's also possible to create smart contracts that can cap the price of secondary market tickets, stop scalping, and give the seller a cut each time a ticket is resold, which could present a potential windfall for venue owners and promoters.

The next iteration of this concept will likely be members-only clubs that issue NFTs as exclusive tokens of membership. This gives members two advantages. First is the ability to sell their membership to someone else. Second is public membership bragging rights because they can display their NFT online either in the metaverse or on their social media. These NFTs will become a social status symbol in the same way a Ferrari or a Patek Phillipe watch is for many people now in the real world.

A good example is the FlyFish Club in New York, helmed by CEO David Rodolitz—a promoter we used to do a lot of business with at JoonBug—and billed as "The World's First NFT Restaurant." FlyFish Club is a members-only club expected to open in 2023. Memberships can only be purchased with NFTs, although food and drinks will be paid for with U.S. dollars.

In Miami, E11EVEN Group, which runs a large hybrid nightclub, strip club, and condominium living concept, has already embraced the concept with E11EVEN Crypto and E11EVEN Captain's Club. Their tagline is "Non-Fungible Nightlife" and you can buy and sell them on popular NFT marketplaces such as OpenSea. Some of the NFTs are selling for as much as 35 ETH (approximately $60,000 as of early September 2022)!

Although it's not a physical club, this is already happening with the Bored Ape Yacht Club. BAYC is an NFT collection where NFT holders get exclusive access to events (both online and offline) and other bragging rights. These NFTs have sold and continue to sell for millions.

The next phase of the nightlife industry is moving the experience from "in real life" (IRL) to the metaverse. The underpinning of this has already begun during and post-pandemic, with people paying to get into virtual Zoom nightclubs with exclusive DJs where only beautiful or popular people are invited. Nightclubs and events in the metaverse will be much like this, but even more immersive.

First, you will likely be wearing a headset à la Meta or Apple, and perhaps a body suit with shoes and gloves that give you haptic feedback.

Next, you'll have a large choice of virtual venues to visit. Different areas of the metaverse will be more popular and cater to different types of crowds. Some metaverse land and properties are already selling for millions of dollars on the major platforms, such as Decentraland and Sandbox. (Although there are currently a few major players angling to *be* the dominant metaverse platform.)

Third, when you enter the metaverse, you will be required to connect your wallet, which will serve as your digital identity. Your wallet will have a reveal of all your NFTs and past purchase history, showing your clout as a super fan or your wealth. It will divulge your preferences like a browser cookie. Instead of pulling up to a club in your exotic car, with your fancy watches and jewelry and designer clothes, you'll pull in with your wallet and everyone will know exactly who you are and what you have.

Club staff will figure out where to seat or place you in the club based on your status. They'll access your wallet and record your loyalty based on how much you spend and frequent the club. You can even instantly pay your bill out of your wallet in crypto at the end of your visit (which can now be at any time of day or night). Once you leave, owners and promoters can easily contact you (and every person who has ever been to their party or club for that matter) because they know your wallet address. It will be game-changing from a marketing perspective and sending customized invites to future events.

You can buy virtual bottles of alcohol that will further serve to show your status in the club, just like people do now, although it would only be for show—unless you plan ahead so that the club can send you the alcohol beforehand, like a Zoom cooking class. And I would imagine much later in the future there will be a way to simulate the alcohol through your body suit or simulated taste and smell.

There could also be real-time apps running in the background of the metaverse which can enhance your experience even further. Imagine a Tinder app running in the virtual club that can help match you up with others who share your interests, or potential dates based on AI matching of your wallet to others.

Eventually, your digital identity will become much more important than your real-life identity.

In-person nightclubs will fall into the realm of the "unhip" or "old fashioned." After the revenge partying and travel dies down from COVID, people will be getting back to more convenient at-home experiences. It will be the opposite of "Netflix and chill," because you will be partying, dancing, spending money, getting drunk, and even hooking up virtually. The number of IRL nightclubs will decline a lot, but some will still be there for the novelty of it, the same way that movie theaters continue to persist.

Nightlife Lessons Learned

The only constant in the universe is change. If you don't embrace the future and adapt accordingly you will soon find yourself obsolete and out of business. This is true in the nightlife business more than most industries because it's driven by young early adopters who are willing to take risks that other more conservative businesses are not. The intense competition to outdo each other and be the coolest drives innovation in entertainment. That's why the metaverse will be driven initially by nightlife before it penetrates mainstream daily life.

APPENDIX

Nightlife Lessons Cheat Sheet

- Persistence Beats Resistance and Fake It Till You Make It.
- Exclusivity doesn't pay the bills!
- You're selling a feeling not a product or service.
- You're only as good as your last success or failure. If you recently had a big win, you have to work hard to win even bigger. If you recently had a big failure, you can still turn it around.
- If you can't buy it then build it. Others will likely need it too and will value what you build. It can either enhance your current business or lead you down the path of a totally new business.
- Whatever can go wrong will go wrong. Figure out how to fix and avoid the problem so it doesn't happen again. But know it's temporary, remain equanimous, and get back to work.
- Everyone (including your haters) will love you for the right price.

- You never know what will happen (good or bad). But be confident you can figure things out, and it will all be OK.
- Focusing on an underserved niche is one good path to a successful business and wealth.
- Know when the party's about to end, and have a sustainable plan in place for your own after-party.
- If you don't embrace what the future changes and adapt accordingly, you will soon find yourself obsolete and out of business.

ACKNOWLEDGMENTS

PUTTING THIS BOOK TOGETHER HAS been a process of walking step by step through a decade that took me from barely out of college to serial entrepreneur, from a young and single nightlife enthusiast to an older and wiser businessman, husband, and father. It's brought back memories and experiences that ranged from hilarious to poignant, from excruciatingly painful to absolutely exhilarating. I'm grateful for those memories, and for the people then and now who have helped me put them down in this book.

First, I'd like to thank my wife, Diane, for supporting my idea to write this book, and for encouraging me in all my endeavors. Thank you for being there, and for patiently helping me out, chapter by chapter, with your English Lit major skills! You rock my world every day.

Thanks also to my sister Kate Bernstein, for being the smartest person in the room—not to mention the most incredibly talented, two-time Emmy Award-winning writer and producer. I am eternally grateful to you for graciously agreeing to edit this book.

To Ariana Gordon Stecker, thank you for being my partner at JoonBug and a big part of its success. Thanks for taking the time to refresh my memory about some of the stories behind this book, and for going into storage and pulling out our old JoonBug press kit, photos, and other memorabilia, which were super useful to me.

Many thanks to Pako Dominguez and Will Ragozzino, two prolific JoonBug photographers who kindly went back and dug up almost 200,000 photos from back in the day. Those photos are now posted on my blog for all to enjoy. Thanks a million, guys!

I'd also like to thank Brooke Uris, who was my right-hand woman for about five years at JoonBug; thanks for also helping me remember so many crazy stories and funny episodes from the wild JoonBug ride, and thanks especially for being the most loyal and amazing employee ever.

To Josh Malin, our JoonBug CMO, and John Surdowski, our digital designer—you guys filled in the blanks on so many stories and details. Thanks for everything, then and now!

Jared Shapiro was essential in laying the foundation for this book by helping me write my first blog entry for my website entitled: "The 12 Things I Learned From the Nightlife Business that Prepared Me for the Real World."

And to the many others who helped me to remember things when I was stuck, especially Bill Spector, Artan Gjoni, Richie Romero, and Redd Stylez: Thank you all! Cheers!

ABOUT THE AUTHOR

SHANE NEMAN IS A SERIAL entrepreneur, venture capitalist, and real estate developer. After dropping out of NYU Medical School and failing at his first startup during the tech-bubble bust of the early 2000s, Neman started over. He built his second venture, JoonBug, into a multimillion-dollar digital events powerhouse that thoroughly disrupted the outdated events and hospitality industry. He subsequently founded a successful SaaS business, EZ Texting, the largest business SMS software platform in the United States.

Now, as a venture capitalist, Neman is a prolific backer of startups, including Impossible Foods, Athletic Greens, SandboxAQ, Cirkul, Flexport, Convoy, Prose, Kraken, Obe, Deep Sentinel, Anvyl, Future, MapAnything, VinePair, Hyperice, and Gupshup.

He is also an investor, developer, and manager of various real estate properties from commercial shopping and industrial centers to large residential buildings, running a portfolio of over twenty properties in major metropolitan cities across the U.S. Although a lifelong New Yorker at heart, after thirty-eight years Neman moved to South Florida, where he currently resides with his wife and kids.

For exclusive outtakes from the book, including thousands of party photos, visit: **WWWW.NIGHTLIFELESSONS.COM**

SHANENEMAN.COM    **SHANENEMAN**   ⓘ **SHANENEMAN**